D0911074

TOGETHER AS A COMPANIONSHIP

The title of this book,
Together as a Companionship,
is taken from "The Union of Minds and Hearts,"
a document of the Thirty-second General Congregation
of the Society of Jesus.

TOGETHER AS A COMPANIONSHIP

A History of the Thirty-First, Thirty-Second, and Thirty-Third General Congregations of the Society of Jesus

JOHN W. PADBERG, S.J.

The Institute of Jesuit Sources
Saint Louis
1994

Number 15 in Series IV: Studies on Jesuit Topics

First Edition

©1994, The Institute of Jesuit Sources
3700 West Pine Boulevard
Saint Louis, MO 63108
Tel.: 314-977-7257
Fax: 314-977-7263

All rights reserved

Substantial portions of the histories of the Thirty-first and Thirty-second General Congregations first appeared in a somewhat different form in *Studies in the Spirituality of Jesuits* vol. 6, nos. 1 and 2 (January–March 1974) and vol. 15, nos. 3 and 4 (May–September 1983).

ISBN 1-880810-08-5

CONTENTS

Preface

In the history of the Society of Jesus, thirty or thirty-five years in and of themselves are not a long period of time. Yet perhaps only the thirty-five years and three general congregations during the generalate of Claudio Aquaviva from 1581 to 1615 have equaled in intensity and change the thirty years that have characterized the last three general congregations, from the beginning of the Thirty-first in 1965 through the Thirty-third and to the imminent opening of the Thirty-fourth in January 1995.

That last generation in the life of the Society richly deserves its full history, as do the three general congregations of those last thirty years. These pages present such a history of the Thirty-first, Thirty-second, and Thirty-third General Congregations.

Yet, properly speaking, such a full history, either of the Society itself during the last thirty years or of those gatherings, cannot yet be written. The events are too recent. The varying and long-range importance of the activities and decrees of the congregations cannot yet be fully assessed by evaluating the impact they have had in the Society. But impact they surely have had. The reality signified by the symbolism of certain of the actions of those congregations is still open to a variety of judgments. Some of the participants in the congregations have written sketches of all or parts of them. But a full and nuanced judgment will demand further research in order to bring into the picture the full spectrum of the background, presuppositions, contexts, interactions, of participants and external agents alike. Perhaps most central to the difficulty of writing about these recent congregations is what makes such writing so necessary; namely, that, at least in this author's judgment, they have been by far the most unusual in the history of the Society. For that reason especially they deserve this first attempt at a history.

The material for these pages comes in part from the *Newsletter* put out by the congregations, itself a significant departure from the complete secrecy imposed while past congregations were still in session. For the Thirty-first Congregation *Woodstock Letters* published a variety of accounts, articles, and letters; especially for the first session it published a series of letters written from Rome originally by a delegate from the French Canadian Province, in which the delegates become not simply representatives of the Society legislating in assembly for its well-being but individual Jesuits personally acting in and reacting to a gathering of fellow Jesuits as a whole and as individuals. Unfortunately, *Woodstock Letters* ceased publication before it could present similar letters from the second session. For the Thirty-second Congregation the author could also draw on his own personal experience as an elected member of the congregation. The account of the Thirty-third General Congregation, and especially the history of its antecedents in the years following the previous such meeting, the illness of Fr. General Pedro Arrupe, the intervention by Pope John Paul II in appointing his personal delegate, Fr. (now Cardinal) Paolo Dezza, fall even more greatly under the difficulties of immediacy noted earlier in these pages than do the Thirty-first and Thirty-second Congregations. For that reason, the account here presented of the last congregation is simply a reprinting of the official "Historical Preface" to its decrees. In the years, or perhaps decades, to come, the details necessary for a more fully developed history of that meeting may be learned.

But history does not stop at an individual last event in a series. So, just as the history of the Thirty-third Congregation carried forward the history of its two predecessors, so also that last congregation has continued on through its reception into the body of the Society and among the Jesuit provinces, communities, apostolates, and individual members. The most comprehensive account of that reception is the letter on the subject written by Fr. General Peter-Hans Kolvenbach to the whole Society on March 3, 1985. It is here included as part of that ongoing history. In 1984 Fr. Kolvenbach had asked superiors and province consultors to tell him "of the Society's reaction to the Thirty-third General Congregation." His account is based on the "more than 1500 letters . . . plus numerous conversations and many meetings at all levels . . . [and] it opens up certain perspectives in the future which deserve our close attention."

Those perspectives are laid out quite clearly and thoughtfully in the letter. Among the most important that he cites are our way of proceeding now: poverty and preference for the poor with Christ; the continuing integration of the service of faith and the promotion of justice in one single mission; apostolic discernment, both difficult and necessary, and the planning that should result; and other challenges to the Society of Jesus. Among these challenges are "the need for each Jesuit to regain apostolic openness in his life and his work"; a frank and serious collaboration with each other and with our coworkers, especially the laity; the effective promotion of vocations; the "rediscovery of the apostolic vocation of the Brothers"; and "the need—itself an apostolic one—for in-depth formation." The Thirty-fourth General Congregation, in turn, will have to take those perspectives into account in its deliberations.

Finally, and above all, the decrees themselves of the three congregations whose history is presented here give, better than anything else, a sense of the uniqueness and importance of those gatherings. The reader of this history is often in the following pages referred to those decrees. They bear reading and rereading as witness both to a solicitude for the history and heritage of the Society of Jesus and to a resolute facing of a future in which that heritage can continue to inspire us imaginatively, as the preamble to the Jesuit Constitutions puts it, "in conformity with our Institute, along the path of divine service on which we have entered" (Cons., [134].

GENERAL CONGREGATION 31

Session I, May 7–July 15, 1965: 224 members
Session II, September 8–November 17, 1966: 226 Members

Introduction

Vatican Council II was holding its third session when John Swain, vicar general of the Society, sent out on November 13, 1964, the letter convoking the Thirty-first General Congregation of the Society of Jesus. The fourth and final session of Vatican II was yet to be held, but the council's influence had already permeated the Church in a way that both enthusiastic advocates and worried opponents could never have imagined only a few years earlier. The Society of Jesus had felt those influences, too; but before much longer it was to feel them even more intensely.

Beginnings

On May 7, 1965, the congregation got under way after the delegates had been received in audience by Pope Paul VI.[1] All the members were present,

---

[1] The decrees of this congregation can be found in "Decreta Congregationis Generalis XXXI," *Acta Romana Societatis Iesu* 14, no. 6 (1961–66): 806–1020, and in a separate volume with the same title, published in Rome in 1967 by the curia of the Society of Jesus. English Edition: *Documents of the 31st and 32nd General Congregations of the Society of Jesus*, ed. John W. Padberg, S.J. (St. Louis: The Institute of Jesuit Sources, 1977). The *Woodstock Letters* (hereafter abbreviated *WL*) material can be found in the following articles: Joseph M. Kakalec, S.J., "The Thirty-First General Congregation," *WL* 94, no. 2 (Spring 1965): 153–64; Pedro Arrupe, S.J., "A Letter of Very Reverend Father General to the Whole Society on the Thirty-First General Congregation, *WL* 94, no. 4 (Fall 1965): 365–71; George E. Ganss, S.J., "Impressions of the Thirty-First General Congregation," *WL* 94, no. 4 (Fall 1965): 372–95; Edward J. Sponga, S.J., "The General Congregation: Its Atmosphere and Hopes," *WL* 94, no. 4 (Fall 1965): 396–406; James P. Jurich, S.J., ed., "The Thirty-First General Congregation: The First Session, *WL* 95, no. 1 (Winter 1966): 5–79; idem, "The Thirty-First General Congregation: Between the Sessions," *WL* 95, no. 4 (Fall 1966): 467–90; "Letters from the First Session," ed. James P. Jurich, S.J., *WL*, Part I, 96, no. 1 (Winter 1967): 5–34; Part II, 96, no. 2 (Spring 1967): 143–95; "Letters from the Second Session," ed. James P. Jurich, S.J., *WL* 98, no. 1 (Winter 1969): 5–32. Unfortunately, *Woodstock Letters* ceased publication before it could

except for several from Eastern Europe. The unprecedented number, 224, strained the housing facilities of the curia. The general sessions were held in the large *aula* arranged for this purpose, but numerous committees met in both the curia and the adjacent House of Writers.[2] Among the delegates at the first and second sessions, the one longest in the Society and professed for the longest time was Severiano Azcona, the Spanish assistant. He had joined the Society of Jesus sixty years earlier, in 1903, and had pronounced final vows in 1921, more than forty years ago. The delegate who had most recently entered the Society was Daniel Pasupasu from Central Africa. He had been a Jesuit only twelve years, since 1953, and in the first session was the most recently professed, as of February 1965, less than four months before the congregation opened. In the second session he was a relative veteran of more than a year compared to Enrico Giraldo from Colombia, professed on August 5, 1966, a little more than a month before the session began.

The vicar general exhorted the delegates "to that peace, harmony, and faithfulness by which this one desire might flourish in such diversity, that the Society of Jesus, faithful to the spirit of its founder, might fully respond to the needs of the Church."[3]

Since there were postulata proposing that the lifelong term of the general should be changed or at least questioned, the congregation thought that in order to "provide for a tranquil election" it ought to consider them beforehand. Hence, the congregation made this its first item of business; and through five sessions it deliberated about two intertwined questions: (1) whether the general should be elected for life or for some determined period (such as fifteen years) and (2), the logically antecedent question, whether the congregation even had the power to legislate at all before it had elected a general as its head. During these debates a solution to the first question gradually emerged, calling for the election of the general for life while providing "cautions" making an honorable active or passive resignation sufficiently easy in case of need. Through a straw vote, consensus on this solution became so manifest that the delegates felt they could now proceed intelligently to the election; and weeks after it, on July 15, 1965, the congregation, how having its presiding officer, voted that solution into carefully phrased law, the present decree.[4] Another question intertwined with the two above was also discussed in those sessions before the election, namely, what the congregation could and could not discuss; for many delegates thought that the congregation was bound by restrictions in the

---

publish its survey of the second session of the congregation.

[2] GC 31, Historical Preface to the Decrees of the Thirty-First General Congregation (hereafter abbreviated as HP, followed by the relevant number or numbers).

[3] GC31, HP 11.

[4] GC31, HP 3; D. 41 [631–41].

Institute forbidding even the discussion of topics pertaining to the substantials. Swain, the vicar general who presided until the election of the new general, toward the end of this debate told the delegates that during a papal audience before the congregation began, Paul VI had assured him that the fathers of the congregation should be absolutely free to discuss anything pertaining to the life of the Society.

The usual gathering of information and other preparations for the election of the general took place in the next four days; and finally, on May 22, 1965, the congregation chose on the third ballot Pedro Arrupe, the fifty-seven-year-old provincial of Japan, originally a member of the Spanish Assistancy and the first Basque since St. Ignatius to be elected general of the Society.

Questions, too, had arisen about the number and duties of assistants to the general. Finally, a plan was adopted that had been strongly supported by Arrupe even before his election as general. There were to be four general assistants, elected by the congregation without regard to territorial designation. There were also to be general consultors, general consultants, and finally, in addition, regional assistants to be appointed by the General. The four general assistants were elected in three sessions. Paolo Dezza, an Italian, had been a participant in three previous congregations, had been rector of the Gregorian University, and was highly respected in academic circles in the Church. Vincent O'Keefe was president of Fordham University in New York; John Swain had been vicar general; and Andrew Varga was provincial of the dispersed Hungarian Province, with his headquarters in New York. "The Europeans, at least some of them, think that the upper echelons of the government of the Society is too Americanized. . . . three of their men belong to the Big Four, . . . Fathers Swain, O'Keefe, and Varga (whom they regard as Americanized)."[5]

The *deputatio ad secernenda postulata* (the committee charged with classifying the postulata), had its hands full as never before in the history of the congregation. More than nineteen hundred postulata eventually came to the congregation, almost all of them on hand as the meeting began. By contrast, the previous congregation in 1957 had received between four and five hundred postulata. Six major commissions were set up: on governance (thirty-nine members, Swain chairman); on the ministries and apostolate of the Society (fifty-nine members, Hervé Carrier, French-Canadian rector of the Gregorian, chairman); on the formation of Jesuits, especially in studies (fifty-four members, Paolo Dezza chairman); on religious life (thirty-three members, George Ganss, St. Louis University and the Institute of Jesuit Sources, chairman); on the preservation and renovation of the Institute (twenty-four members, José Oñate chairman); and on the mission of the Society today, a special commission set up

---

[5] "The 31st General Congregation: Letters from the First Session," *WL* 96, no. 1 (Spring 1967): 153.

by the General, especially in the light of the Pope's request that the Society face
the modern problem of atheism. Each of these except for the last had from
three to seven subcommissions. All of the members of the congregation were
asked to indicate on which group they wanted to serve "in order that the
distribution of the fathers might be done easily and more satisfactorily." Later
other subsidiary commissions were set up; for instance, to help in the actual
writing of the texts of the decrees, to devise better methods of procedure in the
sessions, to answer canonical questions, and to revise the various formulae.[6]

The Procedures

The unprecedented number of postulata, the size of the congregation,
and the recognized need for an expeditious use of time prompted several
procedural rules. At first, each delegate could speak on the same topic of
business only once in a session; later, this was cut down to a speech of seven
minutes' length, and in the second session speeches were limited to seven
minutes if the orator had requested to speak beforehand, otherwise, to only five
minutes. Still, the number of individual speeches was enormous. Red and green
lights on an election board were used in voting. (Toward the wearying end of
the congregation, some of the delegates placed wagers on who could most
quickly attach names to lights.) The *acta* were not read publicly, but distributed
in mimeographed form. But even with such changes in the first session, there
were still vitally important ways of conducting a large deliberative meeting long
in use in the contemporary world that were as yet unknown to or least untried
by a general congregation. A commission on procedure produced suggestions on
these matters for use during the second session. When adopted, for the first time
in a congregation these procedures allowed delegates to raise a point of order
and propose and vote on an amendment to a text being discussed. This latter
was an immense improvement; previously, a text had to be considered, accepted,
or rejected as a whole. Father General was allowed to nominate three vice-
presidents of the congregation; as a result, he did not have to spend day after
day, week after week, presiding over every session of the congregation. For the
first time in the history of this assembly, the second session allowed "open
meetings" of the commissions and subcommissions, open to any delegate and
conducted less formally than the plenary meetings. To help write the *acta* of the
congregation, nonmember Jesuits were called in and allowed to attend full
sessions. Latin was no longer the obligatory language in which speeches were to
be given; English, French, Spanish, and Italian were also allowed. (The Ameri-
cans especially were surprised when a poll of the delegates showed that a greater
percentage understood French than English.) The employment of simultaneous
translation came up for discussion; although not installed for the congregation

---

[6] GC 31, HP 13–16.

as such, it was allowed in the open commission meetings and as an experiment in six of the general sessions. Finally, the rule of ironclad secrecy, in effect for centuries, was abrogated, so that an information office was set up, staffed by nonmember Jesuit experts who attended the sessions and were responsible for the *Newsletter* published in several languages for the benefit of the other members of the Society.[7]

Gradually, the commissions and their twenty-four subcommissions settled down to a pattern of work in which a subcommission of three to seven members would study and discuss the postulata dealing with a particular problem, write a draft decree on the subject, and get it accepted by a majority of its members. Then dittoed copies of the draft would be sent to the thirty or forty members of the full commission. The duplicating and copying facilities at the beginning left much to be desired; as far as long-distance fast communication is concerned, the general-to-be reportedly caused surprise—and puzzlement at what he was talking about—when on his arrival at the curia he asked where the teletype was.[8] (The facsimile machine had not yet been invented.) Commission members returned written comments to the subgroup, which then revised the text *(relatio)*. Then the group submitted the text to all the chairmen of the subcommissions and, after approval by them, distributed it as a tentative draft *(relatio prævia)* to all the members of the congregation. The whole membership in turn had three or four days to submit comments and suggestions for change. The subcommittee then prepared a final draft *(judicium definitivum)* for discussion by the whole congregation at one or more plenary sessions. If that draft was accepted with whatever changes were deemed necessary, it was retouched and several days later submitted to a final vote.[9]

Sessions

The First Session (May 7–July 15, 1965)

All of this procedure was ultimately under the supervision of a board of presidents or chairmen of the several commissions. Obviously, much preliminary work had to be done in the subcommissions; and after the high point of the election of the General on May 22, several weeks were to elapse from May 24 until June 7 before the next general session was held. In that time the all-important work was going on—indeed, "the most important work of the congregation . . . in the private conversations and in the discussions within the

---

[7] GC 31, HP 20. The old rule, in the *Formula congregationis generalis*, no. 25, which was explicitly reaffirmed as late as 1923 during Congregation 27, had said that "no one was to communicate to others outside the congregation the actions taken in the congregation."

[8] *WL*, "Letters," 96, no. 1 (Winter 1967): 88.

[9] *WL*, Ganss, "Impressions," 94, no. 4 (Fall 1965): 387.

subcommissions or commissions."[10] But it was almost inevitable that discouragement should set in, as so little seemed to be getting accomplished finally or definitively.[11] Once the general sessions began again on June 7, the sense of movement returned, only at times to fade into the distance as one speech succeeded another.

One could treat of the material of the congregation day by day, but for the present purposes that would take too long. Instead, what follows will be a short chronological comment, followed by a topical treatment involving both the first and the second sessions; for some decrees were preliminarily discussed in the first session and passed in the second. Suffice it to say here that the congregation made history when it decreed such a second session.

As morale grew with the accomplishments through the latter part of June, so also did fatigue, augmented by the realization that, in the time usually spent in such a gathering, the congregation could in no circumstances complete the work which the Society was expecting of it. The length of the congregation had already encouraged a *boutade* that "the Jesuits from now on have a general *ad tempus* and a congregation *ad vitam.*"[12] By July 1 there was serious concern about what to do: continue on to the end (through the Roman heat),[13] give power of decision to a small group of *definitores*, adjourn and call another congregation in few years, or recess soon and reassemble with the same delegates in a later second session. All these alternatives were discussed. On July 6 a vote was taken, and the decision was made to recess on July 15 and to reassemble in a second session beginning in September 1966. That plan would get the delegates home for needed business and for contact with the members of their provinces eagerly awaiting direct and personal views of the congregation. It would allow a year of further study, reflection, preparation, and discussion. Vatican II would by then have reached its conclusion and the second session could take into account the council's total output.

---

[10] Ibid., 388.

[11] One of the members of the Jesuit curia permanently stationed in Rome took a longer-range view. "Brother . . . marveled [at the peanut butter, supplied by the American delegates as a supplement to the meager continental breakfast]. 'It always does some good to have a general congregation. After the last one, we had an apple at breakfast. Now they've added a little piece of ham, and next it is peanut butter. This will be something for us who'll still be living here after you're gone'" (*WL*, "Letters," 96 [Winter 1967]: 16).

[12] Ibid.

[13] Even the recently inaugurated Pepsi-Cola dispenser at the curia could not quite overcome the Roman heat, although it was a cause of wonderment to the old-timers there. Even more unusual to them was the presence of the General at these Pepsi breaks. One delegate suggested that Coca-Cola might be "prepared to defray the entire cost of the congregation if the delegates are willing to adopt a decree recommending Coke in all the houses of the Society" (ibid., 34).

In the last week or so of the first session, the delegates found exhilarating the amount of work accomplished. Between July 7 and July 13 alone, the fruit of two months of heavy labor became apparent as the congregation passed the final texts of the decrees on studies, atheism, the office and term of the general, poverty, and the tertianship. In addition, the decree on apostolic ministries was finished. There yet remained, for example, much work to be done on the renewal, understanding, and appreciation of the life of the brothers, on grades in the Society, and, most important, on the spiritual life in the Society, especially in the light of Vatican II.

On the evening of July 14, the night before the end of the first session, an event took place that perhaps had no parallel in previous congregations. On the roof of the curia, the *patres graviores* of the congregation produced an entertainment for each other "in which just about every assistancy played some role";[14] it ranged from skits to songs, to updated versions of classics, to a complete synthesis and parody in a recondite Latin speech of every cliché used in the course of seventy days of speech making, to two tenor solos, one in Basque and the other in Japanese, rendered by Father Arrupe.

On July 17 the Holy Father received the General and his assistants, congratulated them on the first session, and asked of them three things: that the Society be faithful to itself, that it adapt itself courageously to the needs of the times, and that it be true to the Church and the Holy See.[15]

Between the sessions, work would be carried on, with General Assistant O'Keefe supervising the overall preparation for the second session. A list of all the work to be done was prepared, ranging from those decrees that needed only a final definitive vote to others that were only in the first- or second-report stage. Mixed commissions of delegates and experts met frequently in the intervening year in Rome, for instance, and in Paris. The date for the opening of the second session was set for September 8, 1966; before that date the General sent to the superiors general of more than seven hundred orders and congregations a letter requesting prayers for the success of the next session; later he sent out more than three thousand additional copies. In the meantime, a special commission had modified procedures for the session in accord with contemporary insights and practices in order to facilitate the work of the delegates, as described earlier in this paper.

---

[14] *WL*, Ganss, 94, no. 4 (Fall 1965): 391.

[15] *WL*, Kakalec, 94., no. 2 (Spring 1965): 369f.

The Second Session (September 8–November 17, 1966)

The second session began on September 8, 1966. The General had invited the delegates to come early for a triduum if they so wished. He had earlier suggested the triduum and asked who might give it; the congregation responded by asking him to do so. Most of the members were able to be present, and Father Arrupe suggested in the triduum that they imagine themselves as present at the scene described in the *Deliberatio primorum patrum*, that they see as a special character of a Jesuit his instrumentality in the hands of God, and that they ardently seek union in the Society and, specifically, personal union in the congregation. He even recalled the concern of St. Francis Borgia, the third general, that the Society would suffer harm if the members of the congregation of his time did not let bygones be bygones and forget the debates as they left the congregation.[16]

On the opening day he set four tasks for this second session. The fathers were to affirm basic principles in a clear and intelligible fashion, to seek to clarify the concrete application of these principles to the situation of today's world, to search out how to form and develop such a Jesuit as the congregation envisioned, and to build up among themselves and for the Society a sense of understanding of common life and of real community.[17]

The first two general meetings dealt with procedural questions, especially with those mentioned earlier—making it possible to introduce points of order and amendments, and appointing three members of the congregation to share the duty of presiding: Dezza from Italy, Jean-Yves Calvez from France, and George Klubertanz from the United States.

Turning now to a topical view of the decrees of the congregation as a whole, one will come to the best knowledge of the extraordinary accomplishments of this meeting from a thoughtful, prayerful reading of those decrees. What follows here is a brief account of some of the more important or illuminating circumstances in which the decrees were produced, not as a substitute for the actual decrees, but as a help to a greater understanding of them in the light of their history.

---

[16] *WL*, "Letters," 98, no. 1 (Winter 1969): 12.
[17] Ibid., 17.

Issues, Postulata, Decrees

The Institute in General

The commission on the conservation and renovation of the Institute had to face right away the goodly number of postulata asking that it be made easier to change the substantials of the Institute. Others were equally insistent that this process could not or at least should not be facilitated. So the congregation had to deal with numbers 12 to 16 in the *Collectio decretorum* mentioned earlier, which summarized the actions that all the congregations, from the Fifth to the most recent, had taken on the substantials. Two papers were prepared for the first session, but they had not been discussed. In the interval, a draft of a decree was prepared, which the second session dealt with at great length. Here, as in many other instances in the congregation, serious differences became apparent in the way two groups approached the problem of preserving the genuine spirit of the Society, an overriding goal to which both sides subscribed. Briefly, some would find solutions in fidelity to documents and to legal precedents; others would find it in the study of and adaptation to concrete contemporary circumstances. After engaging in involved discussions, the delegates approved the decree on the preservation and adaptation of the Institute. This makes clear a definition of the Institute and of "substantials," abrogates the old decree 13 of the *Collectio* (which is found also in *Epitome Instituti*, no. 22), that is, the detailed list of substantials of the first and second order. Quite simply, it recognizes that the "congregation can declare the meaning of the substantials," that in nonsubstantials "the Constitutions can and sometimes should be changed by the general congregation," and that it is the duty of a congregation "to provide for the continuing adaptation of them to the needs of the times."[18]

Grades

The question of the distinction of grades between the professed and the spiritual coadjutors occasioned in the congregation a more vigorous discussion than did almost any other subject. Some postulata called for an abolition, pure and simple, of the distinction of grades. Others pronounced the distinction inopportune; others wrote heatedly against the norms in use for profession. A good deal of research into the origin, history, and progress of grades in the old Society was carried out. Finally, in the first session, by a series of votes, the congregation decided, first, not to ask that the grades be abolished; second, to revise the norms for profession; third, to recommend to the General that he set

---

[18] GC 31, HP 9; D. 4, n. 3 [52, 54, 55]. The number or numbers after HP refer, as usual, to the section number in the Historical Preface. The numbers after the letter D refer to the number and section of a particular decree. The numbers in brackets refer to the bold-letter marginal numbers in the *Documents* volume published by the Institute of Jesuit Sources.

up a commission to go into the whole question in depth, including the advantages and disadvantages that would accrue if all formed members of the Society, both priests and brothers, would receive the solemn profession.

Between the two sessions, the Vatican II decree on religious life, *Perfectæ caritatis*, and *Ecclesiæ sanctæ*, the subsequent letter of Paul VI, appeared, and disagreement arose whether the distinction of grades was or was not reconcilable with them. Experts prepared papers; at the second session the feeling among some delegates was so contrary to the present state of profession in the Society that speakers strongly urged the whole question to be reopened for discussion. There was even some talk of a third session if this matter should delay the rest of the work. Finally, after all the speaking and a day for quiet consideration and prayer, on October 7 the congregation decided again that the grade of spiritual coadjutor should not be suppressed here and now and that *definitores* should not be appointed to decide the matter definitively; instead, right after the congregation experts would go into the whole question of the grade of profession and let the next congregation deal with it.[19] There was not the least doubt that the next congregation would once again have to confront this issue.

Some asked to have the permanent diaconate approved. The congregation decided against it, but asked the General to work at removing obstacles that would impede its later introduction.[20]

The coadjutor brothers were the subject of a long discussion, which eventuated in no decisions in the first session. In the interval, a new draft decree was prepared. The apostolic nature of their tasks was made clear: They might serve in any office in the Society except for those requiring "jurisdiction" in the technical canonical sense. Social distinctions in Jesuit life were not to exist; the brothers were progressively to participate in consultations; they now had a voice in provincial congregations.[21]

---

[19] GC 31, HP 10; D. 5 [61, 62]. How strong the feeling was among some may perhaps be captured by the account of part of a speech by one of the Indian delegates in the second session: "If non-Christians, inspired by human motives, were able to make such a gesture [the abolition of caste], how is it that we who are Christians and who ought to be inspired by supernatural motives would not dare to abolish the caste system that prevails in the Society?" He then shouted, "Ego dico ABOLENDA EST ista distinctio graduum," and applause followed (*WL* 98, no. 1 [Winter 1969]: 25).

Earlier, in the first session, a not untypical remark along the same line held that "we must abolish this title [of grades] which divides the Society into classes, and we must do it immediately" (*WL*, "Letters," 96, no. 2 [Spring 1967]: 169).

[20] GC 31, HP 11; D. 6 [63, 64].

[21] GC 31, HP 12; D. 7 [65–74].

The Formation of Jesuits

On the spiritual formation of Jesuits, more than one hundred and sixty postulata had been submitted. Some of them, of course, vigorously complained about the current training of young Jesuits, as had postulata from congregations of the past. A draft decree was prepared and given to the delegates near the end of the first session. This was a very difficult subject on which to write a decree, and no further progress was made in that session. In the interim, there were many meetings of novice masters and tertian instructors. Taking account of their work, the committee prepared a new draft that elicited quite a few comments. This draft was the subject of one of the open sessions with simultaneous translation. Revisions followed, with the final version noting that it aimed at being "a kind of spiritual pedagogy" and not a doctrinal decree. The congregation voted its approval on November 4, and in the second session it approved a long decree involving both general norms of spiritual formation and particular suggestions for all the stages of formation, with a special note that this formation was an ongoing process, which ought to continue even after the completion of formal training.[22]

The training of scholastics, especially in studies, was a subject that attracted about three hundred postulata. The commission recognized quite clearly that while it was willing to recommend changes in decrees of previous congregations, it could not change Church law; and it counseled waiting for the post–Vatican II revision of that law before laying down anything definitive. A further reason for delay was that needs and structures varied greatly in different regions. So the decree here gave general norms, leaving it to a possible new plan of studies and to regional orders of study to offer further specifications. The General, too, received permission to revise decrees of previous congregations, making use of the help of a commission on studies. The decree was approved toward the end of the first session, on July 15, 1965.[23]

There had been some question of discussing the vows of scholastics and dismissal from the Society; but once it became evident that this involved the pontifical law of the Society, the delegates had to ask whether the congregation even wanted to deal with the subject. The majority decided in the negative, and the congregation dropped the subject.[24]

The tertianship as such was not so much the subject of postulata as were the ways in which it was presently structured. A subcommittee of eight tertian instructors, after study of the intent and purpose of tertianship, decided that the external structure which then existed was not a necessity. Indeed, it had

---

[22] GC 31, HP 14; D. 9 [75–140].

[23] GC 31, HP 14; D. 9 [141–87].

[24] GC 31, HP 15.

grown up over the centuries through the ordinances of congregations and
generals in response to particular circumstances, and could be changed with a
change in those circumstances. In addition, the delegates clearly recognized that
diversity in the various parts of the world where the Society existed prevented
the congregation from realistically setting the same absolute details for the
whole Society. So a decree was proposed reaffirming the importance of tertianship, seeing it as a prayerful synthesis of previous training, a final preparation
for the apostolic life, and an opportunity for the formation of the affections;[25] it
set down general norms on how to renew its structures, approved experimentation, and gave the General the power to decide later, on the basis of the norms
and the experimentation, what was to be set down for the whole Society. The
decree passed on July 15, 1965, as the first session was about to come to an end.[26]

The norms for promotion to final vows were gone over thoroughly, for
the general congregation desired "to meet requests of very many postulata that
the claim to profession of four vows should be based more on the overall
religious and apostolic capability of a man, supposing, of course, that he has
suitable knowledge of theology."[27] The old details of decree 158 in the *Collectio
decretorum* were reworked, and the new decree set the norms for judging the
aptitude for profession as well as for the grade of spiritual and temporal coadjutor. The congregation also recommended a thorough study and review of the
process for gathering and using personnel reports. As to the ceremony for
pronouncing vows, the congregation entrusted to the General the task of
drawing up a regulation for it, making provision for concelebration at the
pronouncing of last vows, the use of the vernacular in first vows, and the
presence there of at least close relatives, who heretofore had been excluded from
this ceremony.[28]

Religious Life

The whole fourth section of the documents of the congregation deals
with the religious life in general and in detail. The section includes eight decrees
(decrees 13 through 20), some of obviously central importance, such as that on
prayer, and at least one that a person could, at best, call peripheral, on reading
at table.

The commission had planned a longer introduction on religious life in
general, but there was not enough time to accomplish everything; and so the

---

[25] *WL*, Ganss, 94, no. 4 (Fall 1965): 390.
[26] GC 31, HP 16; D. 10 [188–92].
[27] GC 31, HP 11; D. 11 [193].
[28] GC 31, HP 17; DD. 11–12 [193–201].

brief decree 13 was passed on November 16, 1966, the day before the end of the second session.[29]

On prayer, in the first session there was a treatment of the teaching on Jesuit spiritual life, followed by comments and discussion in three general meetings; but time ran out. In the interim many experts in history, spiritual theology, and psychology were queried and their responses were sent to all the delegates. A central point on which opinions differed was the statutory full hour of prayer, which dated from Congregation 4 of 1581. All—both those for and those against retention of this statutory hour—agreed on the importance of prayer that was truly fruitful; but they differed about the means likely to achieve this goal. The second session yielded a draft of a new treatment on prayer to which more than eighty speakers contributed their views in the course of almost five full meetings. The subcommission revised it once again; an indicative vote was taken on the question of the ardently debated statutory full hour. Then came further revisions, discussion, more revisions and amendments, and a vote on November 14, 1966. Then came three more formal appeals for reconsideration of the much disputed section 11, treating the length of time for prayer; two were rejected on November 17, the very last day of the congregation, and one accepted into the text of that section. The decree as a whole does not at all make prayer of less account in the life of the Jesuit; as a matter of fact, it places still greater emphasis upon it, making quite explicit recommendations in certain circumstances regarding time and length and type of prayer, for example, in liturgical celebrations. The congregation did, however, go back in principle to the norms set down by Ignatius and later modified in the times of Borgia and Aquaviva. This modification reads in part:

> 11. The general congregation wishes to remind every Jesuit that personal daily prayer is an absolute necessity. But the congregation, recognizing the value of current developments in the spiritual life, does not intend to impose upon all indiscriminately a precisely defined universal norm for the manner and length of prayer.
>
> Our rule of an hour's prayer is therefore to be adapted so that each Jesuit, guided by his superior, takes into account his particular circumstances and needs, in the light of that discerning love which St. Ignatius clearly presupposed in the Constitutions.[30]

The whole decree as it now stands was adopted by a great majority of voters this last day (decree 14).[31]

There were many postulata on devotion to the Sacred Heart, but what they sought implied long, involved research beyond the scope of the con-

---

[29] GC 31, HP 18:1; D. 13 [202–9].

[30] GC 31, HP 14; D. 14, n. 11 [225–27].

[31] GC 31, HP 18:2; D. 14 [210–37] and HP 31–32.

gregation. Hence, the subcommission first recommended issuing no final decree at all, except for a recommendation that the General encourage further study and promote the devotion. In discussion it became obvious that this did not satisfy many of the delegates. So again in the last general meeting, the fathers approved the text of the present decree.[32]

On chastity, the appropriate subcommission consulted moral and spiritual theologians, canonists, and psychologists and, in the interim, prepared and sent a draft to the delegates. The point of the discussion in the second session was whether in a brief time an adequate document could be written that would satisfy many of the delegates. The majority wanted the decree that resulted, but also wished experts to complement it later by their researches, a task committed to the General.[33]

The so-called "crisis of obedience" in the Society was the subject of postulata, some asking that the congregation reaffirm the Society's principles on the matter, and others asking for clarification of the relation of those principles to the insights of biblical studies, psychology, sociology, and the like. Others asked the General to set up a special commission to study the matter thoroughly. After evaluating a proposed draft decree, the congregation saw clearly that, once Vatican II had ended, a group of experts should come together to deal with this question. Such a meeting of eleven members of diverse opinions and tendencies was set up. The usual sequence of comments, draft to all the delegates, further comments, and final draft followed. Many of the delegates did not approve the present version, which omitted what is now in section 10, treating of the obligation of fidelity to one's own conscience and outlining how to deal with the matter if such an obligation was in opposition to the superior's will. On November 11, the decree without that section was voted on. Then on November 12, the delegates approved inserting into the decree the present section 10.[34]

To fashion the decree on poverty involved more time, effort, and perhaps debate than almost any other issue confronting the congregation. The two previous congregations had set up post-congregational commissions to deal with the question. Experts on this knotty topic, working for several years under Father Janssens's direction, had prepared extensive position papers for the present congregation. Aided by these, the subcommission then worked out a multiple-section report, most of which was incorporated into the final decree. The most controverted points in the report dealt with the vow not to relax poverty, the fruit of labor, and the gratuity of ministries; but the whole decree underwent extensive debate, and convictions and feelings on all sides ran very

---

[32] GC 31, HP 18:3; D. 15 [238–42].

[33] GC 31, HP 18:4; D. 16 [243–67].

[34] GC 31, HP 18:5; D. 17, especially n. 10 [278–79].

deep. As to the special vow taken by the professed not to relax poverty, after thorough but indecisive historical investigation, the congregation bypassed the long-debated and virtually insoluble problems by deciding authoritatively that henceforth "in virtue of the vow the solemnly professed are obliged only to this: not to grant a stable income to professed houses and independent residences, notwithstanding other more general expressions which are found in the same declaration" on the *Constitutions,* [554].[35]

Since 1824 the Society has enjoyed a dispensation to accept monetary recompense for its works, and this dispensation functioned as something of a symbol in the discussions on the fruit of labor and the gratuity of ministries. As recently as 1957 the provinces had been questioned as to whether they could function financially if they no longer accepted Mass stipends. Fifty-two out of fifty-four replied no. The question was very bluntly asked: "What does it mean to have a dispensation from a law for one hundred and forty years and—something which is more serious still—*without any hope of returning to the law?*"[36] On the other side, the proponents of no change continually cited the supposed wishes of St. Ignatius, the texts of the *Constitutions,* and the decisions of previous congregations. At one point, after a determined resistance to change on the part of delegates from a particular province, a speaker from another province told them that they should then stop relying on the help they received from other provinces, stop asking that their scholastics be educated gratis in other provinces, and stop suggesting that a central common fund should be set up, because the money needed would "come from forbidden fruit, that is, the revenues of the work done by members of other provinces."[37] One delegate who was becoming discouraged by the length and complexity of the debate found solace in this thought: "The veterans—those who had taken part in previous congregations—tell me: 'You haven't seen anything. In 1957, it was ten times worse, and that debate lasted three weeks, without coming up with any solution.'"[38]

Finally, the vote on the final draft of the decree on poverty was held on July 10, 1965. The expert, Antoine Delchard from France, who had worked to prepare the groundwork on this subject both before and during this congregation, told the assembly that if it withheld its approval, then the whole question was back to the zero mark. The material of the decree was carefully divided into parts so that everyone knew exactly what was being voted. As a

[35] GC 31, HP 18:6; D. 18, n. 14. See also the perceptive footnote 4 in Ganss's edition of the *Constitutions,* p. 253. As he well remarks, "[T]he matter covered by the promise is determined juridically not by what Ignatius meant but by the authority of a general congregation."

[36] *WL,* "Letters," 96, no. 2 (Spring 1967): 161.

[37] Ibid., 168.

[38] Ibid., HP 165.

result, it took fifteen distinct votes to pass what is the present decree. At the actual voting, the great surprise was how small the opposition was. Apparently, in the opinion of some, it never exceeded 10 percent, several times it was only 5 percent. This minority had, in good faith and honest conviction, long and effectively employed its efforts, its tenaciousness, and its repeated formal appeals for reconsideration to block any changes in the legislation on poverty to meet modern circumstances. On the other side, many of the delegates shared the conviction of one of the principal experts who had been working on the question for years, namely, that "this congregation has accomplished more than any other one in the past four hundred years."[39] Three days later the delegates approved the idea of four *definitores* who, with the General, were to draft a document for the adaptation and revision of the legislation on poverty, for experimental use until the next congregation.[40] Since the decree touched the Formula of the Institute of the Society, the congregation informed the Holy Father, who heard the opinion of the Congregation for Religious. By letter of June 6, 1966, this document was approved and confirmed.[41]

On community life and religious discipline, there was no opportunity to discuss the draft decree in the first session. In the interim, there were a new report, consultation of experts, comments, and a new draft. During a discussion in September 1966, it became clear that the delegates wanted another revision. So the subcommittee reworked the text again. The draft came up for discussion again in November, and the congregation approved it on November 17, in its last two sessions.[42]

The subcommittee on knowledge of the Institute thought that reasons advanced in postulata for changing the current directives for reading at table, in the light of diversity of circumstances in the Society, should be dealt with by the General, so it turned the matter over to him. They asked him to see to it that any changes made would not bring about a decline in knowledge of the Constitutions.[43]

Anyone looking back at the eight decrees that make up the work of the congregation as it dealt with religious life is struck by the amount that was accomplished to face the realities of the present day and still to do so within the framework of the history and tradition of the Society. Perhaps here most notably is verified the central characteristic of any successful renewal—historical

---

[39] Ibid., 179.

[40] GC 31, HP 18:6; D. 18 [283–311].

[41] GC 31, "Documents Pertaining to the General Congregation," Document 3, pp. 325–26.

[42] GC 31, HP. 18:7; D. 19 [312–57].

[43] GC 31, HP 18:8; D. 20 [358–59].

continuity and contemporary discernment. These were only decrees, of course; this success would be tested by how they were lived out.

The Apostolate

The Society of Jesus was not founded and does not exist primarily for itself or even for its own members. Its end is twofold: The Society exists to help its own members grow in the love and service of God. But each should remember that "he is a member of the Society founded chiefly for this purpose: to strive especially for the defense and propagation of the faith and for the progress of souls in Christian life and doctrine."[44] Therefore, as a matter of course, the apostolate exercised by the Society should come in for long and serious consideration by this congregation, just as it did in past assemblies.

As to the Jesuit priestly apostolate, some postulata contended that members of the Society had involved themselves to too great an extent in the temporal order, undertaking tasks pertaining to laymen rather than priests; and so they asked that the priests of the Society work mainly and especially in the ministry of preaching the word of God and administering the sacraments. Exactly to the contrary, others asked the congregation to declare quite explicitly that the priesthood in the Society could be exercised legitimately not only in the direct care of souls but also in works ordered even if only indirectly to the good of the Church, works such as scholarly research, education, social ministries. The commission on the mission of the Society in the contemporary world prepared a draft decree that the delegates deemed unsatisfactory. During the fourth session of the Second Vatican Council, the delegates held special meetings with some of the Jesuit experts present there; and with their help several of the delegates prepared a position paper to be sent to all the members of the congregation. Comments followed. In the second session, a special subcommittee was formed to deal with this question of the priestly apostolate. It undertook a revision of the whole draft of the decree, and it was this revision which, after a few changes, the congregation approved on October 19, 1966. A little later there was a request for clarification of what responsibilities ordination itself conferred, and this was furnished on November 7 in section 6 of the decree.[45]

To be considered in conjunction with the above decree were the two decrees preceding it, the first on the better choice and promotion of ministries and the other on the commission to be set up specifically to promote such a better choice of ministries. The first of these commissions set down the sources in which to look for norms of renewal, the dispositions required for such adaptation, cooperation with others in the apostolate, and some fields that in

---

[44] "The Formula of the Institute of the Society of Jesus," [3], in *Constitutions.*

[45] GC 31, HP. 20; D. 23 [386–412].

the circumstances of the time deserved special attention. Those areas of special attention were higher education, labor and professional groups, the education of youth, international organizations, certain geographical regions that demanded strong apostolic efforts without delay, the "neopagans" in regions that were traditionally Christian (this undoubtedly was influenced by Paul VI's commission to the Society in regard to atheism), and works calculated to implement the mandates of Vatican II.[46] The second of these decrees ordered that each province set up a commission on the choice of ministries under the authority of the provincial to aid him to carry out his responsibilities. It also urged interprovincial commissions, either as coordinating groups or as a single body.[47]

More than one question had arisen on the purpose and nature of one of the Society's traditional ministries, foreign missions; and the congregation decided to treat these aspects together in one decree. A commission prepared a draft during the first session, but again there was no time to discuss it. After the session, Vatican II promulgated the decree *Ad gentes* (On the Church's missionary activity), and the apostolic letter *Ecclesiæ sanctæ* followed. The congregation consulted representatives from the whole Society who were experts in missionary work, and then adopted a revised decree on October 22, 1966. A brief decree also dealt with journeys home by missionaries. Several postulata had asked for this, one of them signed by all the Jesuit superiors in East Asia. This too was accepted, with the General and the provincials to set practical norms.[48]

The promotion of the spirit of ecumenism and of work in that area was a natural concern of the congregation, given not only the recommendations of Vatican II but also the Church's increased interest in this apostolate. The usual procedures occurred, position paper, draft, and new position paper in the interim. In the second session a new subcommittee considered not only the comments but also the great variety of regions within which the Society worked and the customs prevailing there. It presented for discussion a revised text. After this exchange of ideas, the General took the unusual step of inviting Cardinal Bea, Jesuit chairman of the Secretariat for the Union of Christians and former rector of the Biblical Institute, to speak to the congregation. After an impressive meeting, a few days later, on November 2, 1966, the delegates approved the decree on ecumenism.[49]

During the first session an investigation into and a discussion of the acceptance of parishes by Jesuits had taken place. In the view of some, regular parochial care in this sense was, if not contrary to the Institute, at least not in accord with it. Two position papers emerged during the interim, one on

---

[46] GC 31, HP 19; D. 23 [360–379].
[47] GC 31, HP 22; D. 22 [380–85].
[48] GC 31, HP 21; D. 26 [414–43].
[49] GC 31, HP 22; D. 26 [444–67].

pastoral institutions, especially the Apostleship of Prayer and the Sodalities (in some places beginning to be called Christian Life Communities), and the other on apostolic work in parishes. After reviewing the comments from the delegates and consulting with the secretariats on the Apostleship and on Sodalities, three separate groups wrote the three chapters of the decree dealing with pastoral services, residences, and parishes. As one commentator remarked, if the operation of parishes was not in accord with the institute, it would be hard to justify the more than twelve hundred parishes entrusted to the Society throughout the world.[50] The decree on these three services and on recommendations to superiors, including one on setting up institutes for the training of directors of the Spiritual Exercises, was passed on November 14, 1966. Because of the changed circumstances in the Church, acceptance of curacies of souls in a parish is no longer to be regarded as contrary to the *Constitutions,* [324, 588].[51]

The apostolate of education occasioned "not a few postulata," asking an explicit declaration that teaching in schools for lay students was an apostolate of the Society in the light of the Jesuit vocation and of more recent theological teachings on the character and office of the priest in the Church. The congregation mulled over the whole matter in the first session. In January 1966 some of the delegates met and prepared a position paper that took account of the work already done on the matter and of comments from directors of studies and experts throughout the Society. This document went to all the delegates and, important as it was, gave rise to many comments, some of them quite directly calling into doubt the general usefulness of this apostolate of education and others seeking solutions for particular problems. In response to so difficult a subject, in a long draft decree the subcommission deputed to deal with the matter tried to incorporate norms not only adapted to our own times but also faithful to decrees of previous congregations.

The second session devoted prolonged discussion to the draft, one of the discussions experimenting with simultaneous translations of the speakers' remarks. In all, about forty delegates addressed the subject and almost sixty amendments were offered to the draft. Near the end of the congregation, on November 12, 1966, it was approved (decree 28).[52] One effect of this decree was the abrogation of the old decree, 141 of the *Collectio decretorum.* As Congregation 21 had approved it, it had prescribed that all professors in Jesuit schools

---

[50] "The First Session," *WL* 95, no. 1 (Winter 1967): 59f.

[51] GC 31, HP 23; D. 27, especially n. 10 [468–94, especially 488–89].

[52] GC 31, HP 24; D. 28 [495–546]. The many amendments to this decree demonstrated the wisdom of the procedural changes for the second session that allowed the introduction of such amendments.

should, if possible, be Jesuits; but if necessity urged otherwise, they could be non-Jesuits if they were of proven faith and virtue.[53]

Probably for the first time, a general congregation enacted an explicit decree dealing with scholarly work and research, and surely for the first time a decree on cultivating the arts in the Society. The question of scholarly research had arisen both directly and indirectly in many postulata. The first session started to look into this; the second set up a special subcommission which in a two-part draft defended such a decree and then established the norms of the decree itself. The archives of the Society provided help in the justification of research, pronouncing it "entirely in accord with the age-old tradition of the Society from its earliest times."[54] The sacred sciences came in for special mention as having "the first claim on the scholarly potential of the Society." But the decree also applied itself to "those sciences which are called positive, both those which look to men and society, and the mathematical–natural sciences, as well as the technical sciences proceeding from then, which profoundly affect the mentality of our times."[55] The delegates approved this decree on November 2, 1966. Some of the delegates had wanted a decree acknowledging the apostolic value of "the liberal arts." A subcommittee looked into the place of arts in the history of the Society and in the doctrine of the Church, especially in the recent pastoral Constitution of Vatican II *Gaudium et spes* (On the Church in the modern world), and contended that the arts may exercise today a great influence, for "they provide a special pathway to the human heart." The decree made specific mention of poetry, music, the theater, and architecture, in which members of the Society achieved greatness. Then the delegates commended and encouraged the whole apostolate of artistic activity, going far beyond simply the liberal arts, something never before done so explicitly. This decree was passed on November 15, 1966.[56] On the same day, a decree was approved that made better provision for the international houses of the Society in Rome, which were directly dependent on the general.[57]

Three previous congregations—the Twenty-eighth, the Twenty-ninth, and the Thirtieth—had spoken of the social apostolate. At this congregation the questions came up with greater urgency, and a decree was necessary in order both to respond to postulata and to bring the then existing legislation on social

---

[53] *Collectio decretorum*, 141; GC 25, 12, 2.

[54] GC 31, 29. From the Jesuit archives came an *Ordination on Training Mathematics Teachers* by Father (Saint) Robert Bellarmine, promulgated in 1539 by Aquaviva (Archivum Romanum Societatis Iesu, *Epp, NN 113*, fol. 184).

[55] GC 31, HP 25; D. 29, n. 1 [547–52].

[56] GC 31 HP 26; D. 30 [553–59]. The decree on the arts surely contributed to the establishment of the various Jesuit institutes on the arts held at different times in the United States and other lands.

[57] GC 31, HP 27; D. 31 [560–68].

matters more up to date and to remedy certain defects in it. Presupposing previous teaching and confirming it, while going beyond it more distinctly in several instances, the congregation passed a decree relatively early in the first session, on July 1, 1965. It reiterated the priorities of Congregations 28 and 29 in this matter, again urged the establishment of social centers, and tried to see that in the course of Jesuit training social dimensions of the whole modern apostolate were taken into account.[58]

Many of the decrees of the congregation referred to the relationship of the Society and lay persons. Some of the delegates, however, felt strongly that there ought to be an explicit decree, especially in the light of the teachings and prescriptions of Vatican II. Finally, near the end of the first session, a subcommission was set up to deal with the proposal. Near the beginning of the second session, the subcommission thought that two decrees would be desirable, one that would treat more generally these relationships and the other that would try to deal with a closer juridical bond of the Society to certain lay people. The objective of this second decree was to respond to the strong desires of some of the delegates to fashion such a bond, a desire, they averred, that was a response on their part to the wish of some lay persons to join themselves more closely to the Society while remaining truly lay. Other delegates seemed to be notably unenthusiastic about the whole matter. In any case, such a provision would touch upon some aspects of the institute, and so a separate decree would be in order. The first and more general decree was passed on October 14, 1966. After much discussion, because of the great differences in the various regions of the world where the Society was at work, the congregation finally approved on November 10, 1966, a brief decree commending the matter to study by the General.[59]

In the light of the postulata on the communications media and the ordinances of the previous general, Janssens, on the same subject, as well as the Vatican II decree *Inter mirifica* (On the instruments of social communication), the delegates early in the first session thought it opportune to issue a decree that would collate and put into order the currently existing norms as well as strengthen the apostolate of the mass media by further commendation and legislation. Certain postulata urged upon the delegates a special mention of the Vatican Radio, an apostolate entrusted to the Society by the Holy See. Finally several postulata dealt with the opportuneness of setting up an information center at the Jesuit headquarters in Rome. All three matters became the subject of separate decrees passed in the first session (decrees 35, 36, 37).[60]

---

[58] GC 31, HP 28; D. 32 [569–79].

[59] GC 31, HP 29; D. 33 and 32 [580–93].

[60] GC 31, HP 30; D. 35, 36, 37 [594–605].

Congregations

A whole section of the work of this assembly dealt with congregations in the Society, preparation for a general congregation, congregations of procurators and provincials, and the province congregation.

Some postulata had asked for general congregations at stated intervals, for example, every six years. The subcommission charged with examining the question finally concluded that the reasons for not having such regular congregations were still as valid as they were when St. Ignatius penned them. On the other hand, the inconveniences mentioned by the postulata could be taken care of, for example, by the congregation of procurators and the congregations of the provinces, the tasks of which were to be enlarged. In addition, the subcommittee declared, the improved communications between the general and the members of the Society made regular general congregations even less necessary. There were those who disagreed, inquiring why, among all the religious orders, the Society was probably the only one that did not hold regular general meetings. They suggested that we had much to learn from such other orders and congregations. Further reasons were adduced for both positions, but eventually on July 14, 1965, the last day of the first session, the congregation decreed that general congregations should not take place at stated times.[61]

Other postulata asked for a reduction of the number of delegates to a general congregation, urging that there should be a more equitable representation of provinces varying vastly in the number of their members, and that the ex officio right of provincials and vice-provincials to come to a general congregation should be subject to revision. Even before the congregation had convened, research into these matters had been done by a specially appointed expert. In the first session there was an abundance of comments on the first position paper, and adaptations in its provisions tried without success to solve what was a very difficult question.[62] Some insisted that any kind of proportional representation smacked too much of political democracy, and that the real question to be considered was not the quantity but the quality of the delegates. This brought a firm reply that what was at stake had nothing do with the civil political order but involved fundamental fairness, that no one could really justify a province of three hundred members having three delegates while another province of twelve hundred members equally had three delegates. Why should the members of the former have a voice effectively four times more powerful than that of the latter? As to numbers of delegates, they had been going up inexorably from the twenty present in the First Congregation. Only in 1923 did the number for the first time reach one hundred, and in just a little more than forty years it had risen to more than two hundred. The second

---

[61] GC 31, HP 31:1.

[62] GC 31, HP 31:2.

session once again witnessed long discussions in several plenary meetings. Finally, on September 22, 1966, the congregation decided that at least for the next general congregation the same norms for apportionment of delegates would apply as then existed.[63] Experience and a good number of postulata convinced the congregation that expert preparation, too, was needed on this issue for a general congregation, and without further ado instructions were enacted for the General and his assistants to take in hand the details of such preparation.[64]

Before the second session began, the decree of the council on religious life, *Perfectæ caritatis,* was amplified by Paul VI's letter *Ecclesiæ sanctæ.* This new document prescribed, among other items, that every religious institute should hold a general chapter within two or three years after the council "to further a suitable renovation" of the religious life of the institute. The delegates, naturally, asked whether Session 2 of Congregation 31 fulfilled that prescription. After hearing a group of six experts, the congregation decided that it was not its place to make such a decision. It asked an opinion of the Sacred Congregation of Religious; and on November 12, 1966, the reply came that the present session did satisfy the provisions of *Ecclesiæ sanctæ,* since it was being held after the specified date of October 11, 1966.[65]

Some postulata wanted simply to suppress the congregation of procurators; others asked for revisions in its structure. Janssens had already had the question researched before the congregation began. The usual procedures by a subcommission followed, and the general congregation finally decided on July 9, 1965, that the congregation of procurators was not to be abolished but revised instead, as described in decree 39, with the addition of a congregation of provincials.[66] In the second session, the subcommission had some new historical information and wanted to reopen the question. Some of the delegates still thought that the congregation of procurators ought to be abolished. The attitude was expressed by one of them, who commented that any institution was pretty useless if in more than four hundred years and sixty-four meetings it had only once called for a general congregation, its sole prerogative. On the other hand, the General remarked that one of the advantages of the congregation of procurators was that it regularly could send to Rome Jesuits whom he had not appointed and who could give him a different view of the state of the Society. In any case, the general congregation refused to reopen the question, and on October 24, 1966, held to what it had decreed earlier.[67]

---

[63] Ibid.

[64] GC 31, HP 31:3; D. 38 [606–15].

[65] GC 31, HP 31:4; letter of Cardinal Antoniutti, prefect of the Sacred Congregation of Religious, Nov. 12, 1966, in GC 31, p. 327.

[66] *WL,* "The First Session," 95, no. 1 (Winter 1967): 26f. and 49f.

[67] GC 31, HP 32; D. 39 [616–23].

For a long time the rules structuring province congregations had displeased many, as the postulata made evident. The mildest epithet directed against it was "gerontocracy," and statistics were cited to prove it.[68] Again, Janssens had already set in motion a study of the problem. The subcommission charged to deal with the question proposed three solutions: a limit on the age of the members of a province congregation, a predetermined set of proportionate age groups in the congregation, and an election of delegates by members of a province. On July 9, 1965, the congregation decided not to abolish the provincial congregation but rather to prepare a reform of the legislation dealing with it. The same number of delegates would be retained, but they would be elected. When the matter came to a vote in the second session, the previous question of whether formally to treat the subject had to be considered since it was part of the Institute. The necessary two-thirds majority agreed to consider it, and on October 22, 1966, the congregation passed the new legislation, adding to it on November 12 the provision that not only could brothers vote but they could also be elected.[69]

Government

On government in general a document had been prepared, but it became clear that questions here would be better treated in the decrees on the religious life, especially in the section on obedience. So no separate decree was written.

For the government of the whole Society, the question of the duration of the general's term of office has already been treated in this history. The congregation confirmed a life term, but made the process of resignation easier.[70] More than one postulatum asked that the General visit the Society laboring in various regions of the world. This would radically change the custom so far obtaining whereby the general journeyed away from Rome only very rarely. The decree was eagerly passed and was implemented by Father Arrupe in the years following the congregation.[71]

---

[68] *WL*, "Letters," 96, no. 2 (Spring) 1967): 174–75. For instance, in New England in 1965, those professed in 1939, twenty-six years earlier, after more than forty years in the Society, were still too young in the Society to attend the provincial congregation. In New York the youngest man in the provincial congregation had professed his vows in 1940, a quarter of a century earlier. One delegate cried out that we should "stop glorifying the wisdom of old men," and reminded the delegates that, in the story of Susanna and the elders, her champion was a young man while they themselves knew what the elders were like.

[69] GC 31, HP 33; D. 40 [624–30].

[70] GC 31, HP 35:1; D. 41.2 [631–41].

[71] GC 31, HP 35:1; D. 42 [642].

Several decrees followed on the office of vicar general and his relation to the general assistants, and on the assistants and consultors of the general. Again, this latter item has already been treated in part. Succinctly put, four general assistants were to be elected by a congregation "to carry out the Society's providence with respect to the general."[72] They were also the canonical "consultors" required by Church law. In addition, there were to be general consultors chosen by the general, regional assistants, and expert consultants. Father Arrupe told the congregation that for this present time he would name as general consultors the four Jesuits elected as general assistants. There was some question of the duration in office of the general assistants, but the two-thirds majority necessary to change the Constitutions could not be gathered, so the term of office remained coterminous with the life of the general.[73]

Official "visitors" had long existed in the governmental structure of the Society. The congregation slightly revised the decree in the *Collectio decretorum* dealing with them. In the course of the discussion, the delegates made clear that they wanted no essential changes, but they did not want "visitors" to stay too long in the province to which they were sent, to stay too long in office, or to enjoy an indefinite authority or jurisdiction.[74]

The government of provinces and houses came in for consideration as a result of many postulata. As usual, they were in some instances at opposite ends of the pole, some calling for more power to provincials and other superiors, others for less. The congregation revised some decrees in the *Collectio* on permissions needed from the general, commended to him the granting of broader faculties to provincials, urged that provincials after some time in office go to Rome to be trained to govern better, and commended to provincials in turn a greater use of expert advice.[75]

Once superiors are appointed to govern, they need help and advice if they are to govern well. So the selection of consultors also occupied the attention of the congregation. For house consultors, provincials were to inquire into and take into account the opinions of members of the community. For province consultors, local superiors were to consult their own communities on their opinions of such consultors, and let those consultors know the results. The same was to be true of house consultors. In all of this, the delegates thought that the Society should accommodate itself to the mind of the Holy See as

---

[72] GC 31, HP 35.3; D. 44 [648–63].

[73] GC 31, HP 35:2, 3, and 4; D. 44 [648–63].

[74] GC 31, HP 35:6; D. 45 [664–65]. One postulatum emphatically asked the Society to "bring to their senses all those disturbers. . . . Let them name visitors to travel through the provinces and throw out these undesirable elements" (*WL*, "Letters" 96, no. 2 [Spring 1967]: 174).

[75] GC 31, HP 37:1; D. 46 [666–71].

expressed in the recent *Ecclesiæ sanctæ*. The decree was passed on November 10, 1966. Later, several delegates made a formal appeal for reconsideration to get the words "vere efficacem" into the first part of the decree, which treats of the members of the Society taking "an effective part in the selection of those who make up councils" (decree 47).[76]

Beyond houses and provinces, there was the question of interprovincial cooperation. Like motherhood, the flag, and the *Summary of the Constitutions*, everyone was in favor of it. But there was great concern how best to translated that attitude into action. The first session took no action, other than discussing the question, because some of the delegates thought that the question was not yet mature. In the second session, on October 25, 1966, the delegates finally passed a decree. It involved such cooperation in general, economic cooperation, and cooperation among neighboring provinces; among other measures, it suggested setting up boards of provincials. Into this decree, too, went some provisions for the establishment and regulation of common houses.[77]

Details

The last set of decrees, involving several specific details of government in the Society, are gathered together in an appendix to the rest of the congregation's documents. The delegates gave the General the power to answer difficulties about and adapt provisions of the various formulae for the several types of congregations in accord with what the present congregation had decreed. Practically, this involved, for instance, how postulata were in the future to be proposed and treated, what ceremonies were to accompany the election of a general, and whether the general congregation actually had deliberative power before it elected a general; furthermore, it introduced changes especially in the formulae for provincial congregations (decree 48).[78]

Censures and precepts were not a popular topic of concern among the delegates. They determined that the whole catalogue of them in the Society ought to be reviewed in the light, not "of fear of offense," but rather "of love and desire of all perfection." So a decree delegated to the General the faculty to review them and to "abrogate the canonical penalties and those precepts that are imposed by the Society's own law." He also could abrogate penalties laid down by the Constitutions and could petition the Holy See for such "abrogation of

---

[76] GC 31, HP 37:3; D. 47 [672–73].

[77] GC 31, HP 37:4; D. 48 [674–94].

[78] GC 31, HP 38; D. 49–52 [695–764]. In the discussion of the ceremonies of election (e.g., the genuflection before the general after his election), it became clear that the delegates did not and could not know either the circumstances of future elections or, especially, how liturgical law was to be changed as a result of Vatican II. So the vicar general was to determine these details when the occasion would arise.

penalties established by particular pontifical law." To realize what a change this was, one must look back upon congregations of the past, which as a matter of course regularly confirmed the censures and precepts then in existence, and often enough added to them.[79]

Just as with censures and precepts, many postulata asked for revision of the directives for censorship by the Society of books written by Jesuit authors. The congregation did not quite know what to do; further research was needed, some delegates said, especially about the doctrines to be held in the Society. This was supposedly to be done by the committee on studies. Then too, the congregation did not know what changes on this matter would appear in the revision of the Code of Canon Law. As a result, the delegates gave the General the faculty to adapt norms of Jesuit law in this respect by way of experiment. It also recommended that boards of provincials propose to the General modifications appropriate to their own assistancy or region.[80]

Finally, in the light of what had been done in the congregation, certain decrees of similar congregations in the past had to be abrogated or revised, so the delegates gave the General the power to do so (decree 55).[81] Similarly, certain positive powers were delegated to the General, as has long been usual in the closing days of congregations. For instance, he was given the power to suppress colleges and professed houses under certain conditions (a very regular and common delegation even though St. Ignatius uses this in the Constitutions as an explicit example of the powers and responsibilities of a congregation), to approve minutes of congregation sessions that could not be distributed, and to make obvious corrections in and edit with regard to style the decrees passed by the congregation.[82]

Conclusion

The Thirty-first General Congregation now drew to a close, to the delight and the sorrow of its participants. Delight because they had accomplished so very much, far beyond their original expectations, and because they were now able to return to their native lands. Sorrow because of the imminent dispersion of a group whose members, for all their real and deep differences, had come to know and respect each other. Just as Pope Paul VI had spoken to the delegates on May 7, 1965, at the opening of the congregation, so now at its end he gave another sign of his interest and affection. On November 16, 1966, the day

---

[79] GC 31, HP 39; D. 53 [765].

[80] GC 31, HP 40; D. 54 [766–67].

[81] GC 31, HP 41; D. 55 [767–70].

[82] GC 31, HP 42; D. 56 [771–74].

before the official conclusion of the congregation, he concelebrated Mass in the Sistine Chapel with the General and five delegates, in the presence of all the other members of the congregation, and spoke of his anxieties about the renewal of the Church and his confidence in the Society.

The next day the Thirty-first Congregation ended, the twelfth since the Restoration. It had held one hundred and twenty-three plenary sessions, in addition to innumerable meetings of committees and subcommittees during the two sessions and during the interim. It had lasted one hundred and forty-one days, seventy in the first session, seventy-one in the second.[83] The very fact of two sessions had made history, but what was much more important is that its accomplishments had made history as well. Beyond that history lay the future—the future of the Society in carrying out the will of the congregation for the service of the Lord, and the future achievements of the subsequent Thirty-second and Thirty-third Congregations.

---

[83] A long congregation indeed but, despite the common impression, not the longest—by four days. That somewhat dubious honor goes to Congregation 8 with its 145 days in one continuous session through the cold of a Roman winter and the glories of a Roman spring, from November 1965 to April 1646.

GENERAL CONGREGATION 32

December 2, 1974–March 7, 1975: 236 Members

Introduction

Although any general congregation of the Society of Jesus is extraordinary, some are more extraordinary than others. In Jesuit legislation, a congregation is regularly convoked not in the ordinary rhythm of every six or so years, as is common in most religious orders, but only after the death of a superior general, in order to elect a new general.[1]

In certain cases, additional general congregations are convoked as extraordinary means of governance, to legislate on "very difficult matters pertaining to the whole body of the Society."[2] Such was the Thirty-second General Congregation, convoked in 1974. In the four-hundred-year history of the Society, it was only the seventh such special congregation. It dealt with serious matters, preparation for which had been more thorough and had occupied the whole Society much longer than was the case before any previous meeting. The cast of characters in attendance as delegates was larger and displayed greater variety than ever before. A part of the media, avid for the unusual, went searching for villains. There was mystery, too, about the source of patently exaggerated accounts during the congregation of what it was doing and how it was reacting. In the course of its deliberations, unusual problems arose. Each of the problems was separable, but they all regularly interacted to provide surprise endings to several distinct acts, all of which came together at last in a resolution to the drama that engaged and still engages the minds and hearts of not only the actual participants in that past meeting but also the members of the present Society of Jesus who attempt to live out the decisions made by the congregation.

This brief history attempts to deal with what happened at that Thirty-second General Congregation. It is all a matter of public record, both written

---

[1] For a general overview of past general congregations, see John W. Padberg, S.J., Martin D. O'Keefe, S.J., and John L. McCarthy, S.J., *For Matters of Greater Moment: The First Thirty Jesuit General Congregations* (St Louis: The Institute of Jesuit Sources, 1994).

[2] *Constitutions of the Society of Jesus,* [680]. Hereafter this source will be cited as *Cons.*

and oral. Only a few of the illustrative examples may be previously unrecorded.[3] Whatever might make this history of the Thirty-second General Congregation distinctive comes partly from seeing it whole and partly from seeing it against the backdrop of what happened in the years since it concluded in March 1975. This is not an account of the motives of the persons involved (for instance, of those who erroneously pictured some of its actions as manifestations of opposition to the Holy See); nor is it a commentary on the legislation produced (for instance, on the decrees "Our Mission Today" or "The Union of Minds and Hearts"). Rather, it is the record of an experience participated in by the members of the supreme governing body of the Society of Jesus, men ultimately responsible before the Lord and to its members for charting its paths to the future. The congregation gave to Jesuits an apostolic task, a source of direction, and integrative principles of community life for a future which the Society has been fashioning for itself ever since as it attempts to serve the Church of Christ and the Lord himself. This history tries to tell how the congregation carried out its responsibilities toward all the members of the Society.

What started the whole process? What did the preparation involve? Who attended the meeting? What issues were to be dealt with, how did the congregation actually function, what problems arose, and what solutions were eventually found?

Preparation and Participants

Preparation

The Thirty-second General Congregation was formally announced by the general, Fr. Pedro Arrupe, on September 8, 1973, in a letter setting the opening date for December 1, 1974. But the roots of the congregation went back further in time. In October 1970 a "congregation of procurators" had met in Rome. Such a congregation, held every three years and consisting of one elected delegate from each province, has the responsibility to decide whether a general congregation should be called. That procurators' meeting of 1970 decided formally not to call for a general congregation. It was the common sentiment that such a meeting was desirable; but according to the law of the Society, if the congregation of procurators formally mandated a congregation at this time, it would have to begin within eighteen months, that is, by April

---

[3] The norms of the Society for general congregations generally allow the subject matter dealt with in a congregation to be known publicly, but particular opinions advanced therein are not to be attributed to specific persons. The outcome of voting can be revealed, but not the number of votes received by different persons. See the *Formula congregationis generalis*, no. 31, 3, in *Acta Romana* 16 (1976): 836. Hereafter the *Acta Romana* will be cited as *AR*.

1972. Everyone, however, considered this too short a time for preparation. Fr. Arrupe made it plain to the procurators that he understood this viewpoint; and so a month later, in November 1970 he announced to provincials the remote preparation throughout the Society for a general congregation to be called later.[4] In giving reasons for calling the congregation, the General said that the years since the Thirty-first Congregation (1965–66) and since the Second Vatican Council (1962–66) had ushered in so many changes to the Society and to the Church and to the world that he considered it incumbent upon him to allow the highest governing body of the Society to submit its present condition to "deep, realistic, and open consideration." Those words were to be important. The congregation genuinely tried to live up to them. It did not always find it easy to do so; and in its attempt succeeded in bringing upon itself from outside criticisms of the very depth, realism, and openness that it was attempting to exercise.

In April 1971 a six-member preparatory commission was set up. Its members were Jean-Yves Calvez (Province of Atlantic France), Parmananda Divarkar (Bombay), Walter Farrell (Detroit), Johannes C. Gerhartz (Lower Germany), Luciano Mendes de Almeida (East Central Brazil), and Tomás Zamarriego (Toledo). During these preliminary steps, during the actual preparation, and during the period between convocation and commencement, the General kept Pope Paul VI informed of his intentions and of the progress of preparation.[5]

No previous congregation in the Society's history had devoted such a lengthy period to preparation. No previous congregation tried to involve in that preparation as many of the members of the Society. What responsibilities that widespread consultation imposed upon the delegates this history will deal with later.

From 1971 to 1974 that preparation went on. According to the rule of the Society, this was the responsibility of the General and his four general assistants, Vincent O'Keefe (New York Province), Jean-Yves Calvez (Atlantic France), Horacio de la Costa (Philippines), and Paolo Dezza (Venice-Milan). After consulting all the provincials, Fr. Arrupe specifically named the previously mentioned preparatory commission to carry on this work. Between October 1972 and October 1973, the General met with all the Jesuit provincials in five different language and geographical groups at Rome (twice), Nice, Mexico City, and Goa. Several hundred Jesuits around the world worked with the preparatory commission in their own local provinces and areas to set up conferences,

---

[4] *AR* 15 (1970): 613.

[5] At Easter 1972 Fr. Arrupe wrote to Pope Paul VI that he intended to call a general congregation in 1974 or early 1975. On April 18, 1972, Cardinal Villot, Vatican secretary of state, acknowledged, on behalf of Pope Paul VI, the General's letter.

assemblies, meetings, and forums on everything from study to prayer, from the Constitutions of the Society to the problems or opportunities of a particular place. All of the preceding preparation was unofficial and it resulted in enough paper work to gladden the heart of a copy-machine stockholder.

It culminated in the "official" preparation of fifteen months which began once the congregation had formally been summoned in September 1973.[6] The opening date of the congregation was set for December 2, 1974. There were, as usual, three parts to that official preparation. They included the drawing up and submission of postulata, or formal requests for consideration (every Jesuit who wished to submit such a proposal had the right to do so), the holding of the province congregations, and the election thereat of delegates to the general congregation, as well as the choice of official province postulata.

How many individual or personal postulata were sent to province congregations is known only to the divine mind, but each of the almost thirty thousand Jesuits throughout the world had the opportunity to make known what he wished the congregation ought to do. This was the first time in the history of the Society that members of a province congregation were elected. This was due to the decisions of the Thirty-first General Congregation. Previously, the forty oldest professed members of a province had automatically become members of a province congregation. As a result of their deliberations on the material which they received, 934 official province postulata went to Rome from the various provinces and vice-provinces of the Society. Sent directly to Rome as joint postulata from Jesuits engaged in particular apostolic works were another eighty-six postulata. Together they made up a volume of more than five hundred pages, one of the first gifts to the men who were to go as delegates to the congregation. More postulata came later during the congregation from the delegates themselves to swell the total number to 1,020. Three special preliminary committees, mandated by the previous general congregation, were appointed to finish the work of preparation.[7]

The delegates to the congregation from each province were the provincial, who served ex officio, and the two professed members elected by each province congregation. Vice-provinces elected and sent only one delegate. The number elected was 148; 88 went ex officio or by appointment, including the General and the 4 general assistants, all the provincials, the regional assistants, the secretary, treasurer, and procurator of the Society, and 4 others named by the General. The grand total then was 236.

If all the details of this preparation may have bored the present reader, so too by the end of four years the lengthy, detailed, and complicated preparation itself may have bored some members of the Society. But in the long run

---

[6] Letter of Convocation, Sept. 8, 1973, in *AR,* 16 (1972): 109–15.

[7] *AR* 14:970.

that preparation was important in itself for the effective carrying on of the congregation and, perhaps even more important, for two other reasons. First, the details of that preparation were a touchstone against which the congregation measured its responsibility and fidelity to its fellow members of the Society. Secondly, those details can serve historians as evidence that, far from being in any way a maverick meeting, the congregation truly did know and did try to express the mind of the Society as it had become clear over a four-year period of consultation, discussion, reflection, prayer, and decision.

Participants

Diversity was as evident as the number of delegates itself.[8] Let us start with the principal members of the curia who took part, and in the first place with the General. Fr. Arrupe was at that time sixty-seven years old and had been general since 1965. He was a Basque of Spanish nationality, had studied medicine, had entered the Society in Spain in 1927, had done his Jesuit studies there as well as in Belgium, the Netherlands, and the United States. For twenty-seven years he had been a missionary in Japan, serving there as the director of novices and, at the time of his election as general, as provincial. The four general assistants came from France, Italy, the Philippines, and the United States. Jean-Yves Calvez had a background in sociology, politics, and international affairs. Paolo Dezza was a philosopher and theologian, former rector of the Gregorian University, and former secretary of the International Federation of Catholic Universities. This was the fifth consecutive general congregation to which he was a delegate. Horacio de la Costa was a historian, former official of the Ateneo de Manila, and former provincial of the Philippines. Vincent O'Keefe was a theologian, a former professor of theology, former rector and president of Fordham University. The secretary of the Society, Louis Laurendeau, was from French Canada; the treasurer, Eugen Hillengass from Germany, had done graduate studies in economics; the procurator of the Society, Pedro Abellán, who was responsible for official relations of the Society of Jesus with the Holy See, was a moral theologian, and had been rector of the Gregorian University and a *peritus* ("expert") at Vatican II. He had attended the three previous general congregations. The twelve regional assistants—of Italy, Germany, France, Spain, the English Assistancy, the United States, the Slavic Assistancy, southern Latin America, northern Latin America, India, East Asia, and Africa—included men who in the Society had been, for example, sociolo-

---

[8] The source for this material on the delegates is the *Elenchus patrum Congregationis Generalis XXXII* (Rome: Curia S.J., 1974); for the members, see also *Documents of the 31st and 32nd General Congregations of the Society of Jesus,* ed. John W. Padberg, S.J. (St. Louis: Institute of Jesuit Sources, 1977), 551–56. Hereafter, this volume will be cited as *Documents.* References to the decrees of General Congregation 31 will be cited as GC 31; those of General Congregation 32 will be cited as GC 32. Texts for these decrees will be found in *Documents.*

gists, directors of the tertianship (or final formation period for Jesuits), university presidents, moral theologians, experts in international law, and principals of secondary schools. Several of them had also previously been provincials.

From around the world, again to give but a few examples, among the delegates were the former editor of *Civiltà Cattolica,* who was now director of Vatican Radio, a former rector of the state University of Innsbruck, Austria, a historian specializing in the Laínez epoch of the Society, the General's delegate for the Byzantine Rite in the Society, the novice director in East Germany, a member of the French worker-priests who was a specialist in industrial electronics, an anthropologist at Louvain, a one-time missionary in Chad, a psychiatrist and professor of spirituality, a rural sociologist, and a professor of Buddhist studies. Several delegates had backgrounds of teaching and research in classical or modern languages and literature. There was a man who had been imprisoned for several years by the Chinese Communists. Two had degrees in chemistry. There were editors of the review *Mensaje,* a specialist in the fields of the philosophy and history of art, and a counselor in a center for the social rehabilitation of adults. Other delegates had backgrounds of study or experience in fields as diverse as nuclear theory and psychology, political science and biology, communications and canon law, anthropology and English literature, educational administration, spiritual direction, and the history of ideas. The academic specialization pursued by the single largest number of delegates was theology or philosophy. History seems to have been the second-largest specialization. A good number had been rectors of houses of formation; and besides those who were currently provincials, a substantial number of those elected had at some time previously held that office.

For the whole Society the age span of the delegates was quite large. The oldest delegate at seventy-three, Paolo Dezza, was more than twice as old as the youngest, Fernando Montes of Chile. The median age, however, was forty-nine. This reflected the overwhelmingly large grouping in the range of the forties and fifties. Almost two hundred of the total were in those two age groups.

New York was the largest province represented, with 1,097 members, and Chile the smallest with 177 members. Several of the vice-provinces in India, with only one delegate, had many more members than several of the full provinces with three delegates. In five provinces or vice-provinces, Hungary, Bohemia, Lithuania, Slovakia, and Romania, provincial congregations could not be held. The Romanian delegate was absent; a delegate for each of the other four had been appointed and was present.

Issues and Postulata

After so extensive a preparation, probably every Jesuit had his own "little list" of what he personally considered the major issues to be treated by the congregation. The official large list of those major issues in a sense took shape of itself out of the number of similar postulata dealing with several particular items sent in from all over the Society. To judge from that five-hundred-page compilation of postulata presented to each delegate upon his arrival, if the number of pages per subject was any indication, the Society was especially concerned about the following items: The question of the "fourth vow" took up fourteen pages; formation and studies in the Society, twenty pages; community life and obedience, twenty-eight pages; the categories of members, thirty-nine pages; the apostolates of the Society, forty-seven pages; and poverty, ninety-five pages.

As it turned out, these major compilations made up a rather accurate forecast of what the congregation's agenda was to be. For instance, the many pages on poverty were occasioned in part by the detailed formal legislation mandated by the previous congregation, in part by concerns relating to Jesuit lifestyle both personal and communal, and in part by the increasingly common distinctions between the operations of a community and of an apostolate. The pages on the apostolates of the Society contained what was to be the extremely important material on the promotion of justice and on the service of the faith, the latter especially in the light of Pope Paul VI's request at the Thirty-first Congregation that the Society occupy itself with the question of atheism. The fifty-three pages on the fourth vow special to the Society and on the categories of members were eventually to be part of one common but complex consideration.

In greater detail, what kinds of issues did the postulata address in each of the areas just mentioned? What were the members asking the congregation to consider and act on, and how?

The Fourth Vow

The "fourth vow," by which the professed members of the Society commit themselves to special obedience to the pope with regard to "missions" upon which he wishes to send them, was the subject of a great number and variety of postulata. Some stressed the fundamental character of the fourth vow, imparting its identity to the Society, and asked that it therefore be highlighted. Others, similarly taking their stand on the importance of this vow for the Society, rather regularly and with some logic asked that all the members of the Society take the vow, therefore, and not only the professed. Even more fundamentally, some postulata asked the congregation to clarify the meaning and scope of the vow. That this was needed was obvious in view of the different interpretations put upon it by the various postulata. Everyone agreed that it applied to particular apostolic ventures or "missions" to which the pope might send Jesuits. But there were some who obviously conceived of it much more widely. For instance, some judged that in some way it conditioned or even required the doctrinal assent of Jesuits to the teaching authority (magisterium) of the Church, and especially of the pope. The question obviously needed careful historical investigation, something that a congregation itself was hardly capable of undertaking. One really ought to know to what he is binding himself when he takes that vow in the Society, and that can only be determined by its meaning when it became an original element of the Society at its foundation, and as it was authoritatively understood throughout its history.[9]

This question of fidelity to the magisterium, especially to that of the pope, came up also in postulata not connected with the fourth vow. In some instances they dealt especially with the thorny question of the freedom necessary for serious and honest theological research, and the equally spiny question of how to deal with the public writing and speaking of Jesuits, especially in regard to the communications media.

The Fundamental Character of the Society

The fundamental character, or the "essentials" of the Society, was a concern for a fair number of postulata beyond those dealing with the fourth vow. But at this point, the questions of the Society's "sacerdotal" character and of its "apostolic" character met and led back to the original question. There was no inclination in the postulata to call into question that sacerdotal character as one of the Society's essentials. At the same time, some postulata asked, if the Society was also fundamentally apostolic, then why should not all the members share in that particularly apostolic fourth vow? Yet, according to the clear statements presently in the fundamental documents of the Society, only priests were eligible for the "solemn profession." These interrelated questions were to puzzle the congregation internally and to be the occasion of simplifications and exaggerations externally.

Formation and Studies

Postulata on formation and studies in the Society exhibited concern for the decrease in vocations, but they expressed much more concern that the quality of formation should not be allowed to deteriorate. For many, the study of philosophy and theology was overwhelmingly central to the academic aspect of that formation. For the spiritual aspect of that formation, worries were

---

[9] See the study by John W. O'Malley, S.J., "The Fourth Vow in Its Ignatian Context: A Historical Study," *Studies in the Spirituality of Jesuits* 15, no. 1 (Jan. 1983).

expressed, as they have been at every congregation including the very first one in 1558, that the formation was not as rigorous as it had previously been. But given the extraordinary changes of the previous several years since Vatican II, there was an encouraging amount of optimism about the ways in which the Society was responding to the mandates of the Thirty-first General Congregation expressed in its documents on the training of scholastics and on spiritual formation. That meeting had stated directly that "the training of the scholastics should be *apostolic* in its orientation."[10] The Thirty-second Congregation was going to emphasize *integration* as its central theme, integration of the individual himself and as a member of the apostolic body of the Society.[11] As an intrinsic part of that program of formation, some postulata insisted not only on apostolic experience but on such an experience based on direct involvement with the life of the poor. This theme was, of course, connected with the related questions in postulata regarding an "option for the poor" in our apostolates and on the promotion of justice as a constituent part of those apostolates.

Community and Personal Religious Life

As has been true for every general congregation of the Society, Jesuits through a variety of postulata gave evidence of their concern for the specifically religious and spiritual life of the Society, In the past, such postulata had dealt primarily and almost exclusively with personal Jesuit religious life. What was somewhat new for the Thirty-first Congregation and for the Thirty-second also was the direct and specific emphasis on the importance of the character and quality of a Jesuit community itself in the life of a Jesuit who was a member of that community, and on the character and quality of his participation in that community life.

First among the specifically religious concerns was the prayer life of Jesuits. Some postulata saw a falling-off in it and wanted definite remedies, perhaps a return to the former rule of a fixed hour of prayer for everyone. Others, while aware of the difficulties of prayer in current circumstances, urged the further encouragement of what they saw as a basically healthy growth in the spiritual life of Jesuits, supported and sustained by community structures. Frequently the postulata commended the decisions of the Thirty-first Congregation on the spiritual life and recommended that the Society carry them out better. This included such items as regular, ongoing personal spiritual direction, the account of conscience, a further deepening of knowledge and use of the Spiritual Exercises, and community support for one's prayer life, including more emphasis on prayer in common than had been traditional in the Society.

---

[10] GC 31, D. 9:1 [141]; emphasis added.
[11] GC 32, D. 6 [133–86, especially 139–40].

There were some frank postulata, too, about the practical failings in the community life of individual Jesuits and in the very structures of the communities themselves. Some asked for a description of what went into the making of a successful community in the way of a shared life of faith, human communication, physical and psychological structures, lifestyle and apostolic witness. The apostolic nature of Jesuit communities was regularly affirmed, and this fundamentally apostolic character of a community, of course, related to the postulata on apostolates.

Some persons outside the Society may have seen, in the changes introduced by the Thirty-first Congregation and continued by the Thirty-second, only a damaging loss of the rules that had helped to structure religious life. Most Jesuits, however, if one can judge from the postulata, saw the changes as healthy and conducive to personal responsibility internal to the Society. Those changes had brought about the disappearance of an anachronistic regimen imposed by collections of rules common to all, and of overly detailed particular rules for everyone from the rector to the keeper of the clothes room. No one wanted to go back to the minutiae of such rules of yesteryear, but some asked for at least a minimum of clear and simple responsibilities incumbent on all Jesuits.

Obedience

Because it is important in the spiritual life of any Jesuit and because it is regarded as a distinctive mark of the Society, there were postulata also on obedience. As in the past, they were often placed in the context either of internal religious life or of the apostolic work of the Society. In the present, two new elements were introduced. The first was the heightened sensitivity to the rights and demands of conscience; the second was the increased emphasis on a spiritual discernment that was both personal and communal. The postulata usually asked for an affirmation of the mutual and interlocking responsibilities of superiors and members and communities in arriving at the point where a superior could and had to make decisions, and for a clear statement of the importance and value for a Jesuit of recognizing that he was being "sent" by the Society, officially and with its support, to a particular task.

"Grades," or Categories of Membership

The unity of the Society and the common goals to which its members had given themselves were important considerations all through the congregation. They loomed large in the postulata and in the concern for "grades" in the Society. Many postulata clearly exhibited the desire for an internal equality of membership in the Society, not only de facto but also de jure. In part, of course, these postulata—as was true of so many others—were an ongoing response to actions of the Thirty-first Congregation. It had quite clearly stated that it had wanted a thorough renovation and adaptation in the Society.[12] The previous congregation had reminded itself and the Society that it was within the competence and power of a current general congregation (and not only of past ones whose decisions had, up to this time, been regarded almost as set in sacrosanct concrete) to declare which matters were substantial in the Institute, that previous congregations had done so, and that it also had the power to declare the meaning of the *Formula of the Institute* itself.[13] Since that was the case, the congregation had asked the then newly elected Fr. Arrupe to set up a commission to investigate thoroughly the whole question of grades for the next congregation, which was to be this present one. In the meantime, social distinctions formerly existent in the Society between priests and brothers were to cease, and coadjutors, both spiritual and temporal, were to have voice in the provincial congregations.[14]

Partly as a result of those actions, postulata now ranged from finally admitting everyone to profession to not accepting any more religious at all into the Society who were not according to present law capable of profession. All of this material touched on the fundamental characteristics of the Society and on documents not dependent upon the competence of the Society but of the Holy See. So it was clear that the thicket of considerations would be thorny, and that if the congregation took up the matter in response to these many strongly urged postulata, it would have to have recourse to the Holy See at some point.

Apostolates

Since the Society existed not for itself but for the service of the Lord and the Church, the apostolates of the Society were a very large item among the postulata. In addition to requests for the reaffirmation of the Society's commitment to various specific apostolates, there was a repeated stress on

---

[12] Sometimes forgotten by older members of the Society or unknown by those who entered the Society since 1966 is the sweeping statement early in the Thirty-first Congregation about such a renovation and adaptation: "Thus it has determined that the entire government of the Society must be adapted to modern necessities and ways of living; that our whole training in spirituality and in studies must be changed; that religious and apostolic life itself is to be renewed; that our ministries are to be weighed in relation to the pastoral spirit of the Council according to the criterion of the greater and more universal service of God in the modern world; and that the very spiritual heritage of our Institute, containing both new and old elements, is to be purified and enriched anew according to the necessities of our times" (GC 31, d. 2:3 [21]).

[13] GC 31, D. 4:3 [50–52].

[14] GC 31, D. 5:2 [61–62] and GC 31, D. 7:6 [72].

certain characteristics or criteria that ought to mark present apostolates or ought to govern the choice of future ones.

Some of those characteristics were the explicitly spiritual dimension of the works undertaken by the Society, and especially the imprint on all those works of the heritage of the Spiritual Exercises; an effective response to Pope Paul VI's request that the Society work with the problem of nonbelief and atheism (the "promotion of faith" was to express this in another positive way); the ecumenical dimension which ought to be present in the Society's apostolates; the internationalization or broadening of the Church and its gospel message from Western European culture to the cultures of other lands ("indigenization" might be the best word to express the thrust of the postulata; "inculturation" was the term which was to come as a result of the congregation's work on this question); the importance of qualified Jesuits engaging in secular occupations or professions, especially in yet developing lands where there were no others to take up those responsibilities; the need for a commitment to the poor in Jesuit apostolates and especially to those poor who were oppressed by social injustice. This last characteristic requested by postulata led inevitably into a commitment to apostolates that could impinge upon social structures themselves. Many postulata recognized fully the danger of misinterpretation of a Jesuit's religious or social activities as direct political engagement. Because the Society has been so much engaged in the educational apostolates, postulata on that subject were numerous. But often enough they, too, looked to concerns that were ecumenical, social, faith-involved, or international. An example of this international dimension was the concern that the international educational institutions in Rome in the care of the Society respond to the needs of a worldwide Church.

Poverty

Basically four interrelated areas of poverty were the subjects of postulata. The first was juridical or legal, the second institutional, the third communitarian, and the fourth personal. The juridical material was in great part occasioned by the commission on poverty set up by the Thirty-first Congregation. At its mandate, *definitores* named by the congregation had worked to "prepare in stages a schema of adaptation and renewal, and revision of our entire law concerning poverty."[15] The revision had become interim law until the next congregation, that is, the Thirty-second, could review and finally approve it.

The postulata on the institutional aspects of poverty were related to those juridical aspects. In general, they dealt with the distinctions between the Jesuit religious community and the institutional works or apostolates served by

---

[15] GC 31, D. 18:20 [310].

that community, and with clear accountability and appropriate control of the separate finances of the two.

For both communities and institutions there was also the question of sources of revenue. Briefly put, from its beginning the Society had made it a rule to ask or accept for its services no payment due in any way in justice or law. It was to commit itself to gratuity of ministries and a dependence upon alms. Once "colleges" started, they could have endowments so that students need not pay for the cost of instruction. After the suppression of the Jesuits, the French Revolution, and the restoration of the Society, Jesuit institutions endowed by towns, kings, bishops, or wealthy laymen were a thing of the past. Without tuition there could have been no Jesuit schools. In the early 1830s the Society received from the Holy See a "temporary" dispensation from this rule of gratuity of ministries.[16] The dispensation lasted until the 1960s, when the Thirty-first Congregation made a distinction between community and apostolate, changed the age-old rule, and allowed for stable sources of revenue for apostolic works. Some postulata at the present congregation wanted to deal again with gratuity and, if not to return to it, at least to try to move closer toward it, although the postulata were not at all clear on how to do so. On the level of the personal practice of poverty by Jesuits, postulata showed some worry about its vigor and effectiveness in daily life. They also saw the practice of religious poverty as part of a witness to the solidarity of Jesuits with the poor.

Governance

On two levels postulata dealt with questions of Society governance. The first was on the level of the whole Society, the second on the more provincial or local level. For the whole Society several questions arose. The first dealt with the advisability of periodic general congregations. There was also the frequently expressed request that participation in province congregations should not be limited only to those with final vows, as was currently the case. This last provision was itself an expanded participation made possible by the Thirty-first Congregation. Hitherto, participants included, besides the ex officio members, only the forty oldest professed members of a province. A "gerontocracy" is what some had rather wryly dubbed it. The Thirty-first General Congregation had introduced for province congregations the election of and by members with final vows. Some postulata asked this present congregation to broaden participation to include in some way Jesuits who did not yet have final vows.

Other postulata asked for a review of the structure and effectiveness of the central government of the Society. Such a review of the structures newly

---

[16] The distinction of thus making tuition charges possible in Jesuit schools goes to St. Louis University. This institution received the original dispensation, upon which all other Jesuit schools depended in this matter until the Thirty-first Congregation.

put in place by the Thirty-first Congregation had been foreseen as desirable when the next congregation would convene. For the whole Society, too, several postulata again brought up the question of a limited term of office for a general. Whether these latter postulata in any way would have gained support in the congregation really cannot be known because, by the time the misunderstandings with the Holy See had come upon the congregation, there was every desire among the delegates to support the General, Fr. Arrupe, and any question of a limited term might at that time have seemed a reflection upon him.

The Congregation in Session

Beginnings

On the morning of December 2, 1974, Father Arrupe opened the Thirty-second General Congregation with an address in which he quite directly said that the calling of the congregation was the greatest decision of his generalate. He described the overall attitudes with which the delegates had to approach their work. There was a common responsibility to the Society to take practical decisions on structures, spirituality, formation, and apostolates in the light of the needs of the world, the expectations of the Church, and the resources of the Society. There were expectations from the Jesuit brethren who had chosen the delegates. And in the midst of all the work to be done, said Fr. General, there was a single unwavering basis for confidence and serenity, namely, the Lord.

Two innovations introduced by the previous congregation became a regular part of this present gathering. Simultaneous translation, employed hesitantly, partially, and experimentally in the second session of the Thirty-first Congregation, became a regular and fixed part in the Thirty-second. An office of information prepared and published regular bulletins in five vernacular languages. This office also had its work to do in answering questions from journalists worldwide, sometimes in response to rumors and misinformation.

The recourse to the Lord of which the General had spoken was symbolized and expressed in a deeply moving celebration of the Eucharist that same night of December 2. All the delegates, in addition to more than five hundred Jesuits resident in Rome from all over the world, gathered at the Gesù for the liturgy. That principal church of the Society, its interior splendidly illuminated, had never better embodied the baroque desire to celebrate the glory of God in the beauty of human artistry. The gathering of Jesuits ranged from the oldest members of the Roman houses to Jesuit students of every continent and tongue to Italian novices, whose blue jeans were a counterpoint to the lapis lazuli on the great memorial altar dedicated to Ignatius.

On the next day, December 3, Pope Paul VI received all the delegates in the rather overwhelming magnificence of the Consistorial Hall at the Vatican. At many previous congregations, the oldest delegates from each assistancy customarily made up a group that went to the pope to tell him formally that the congregation had begun and to assure him of the Society's readiness to respond to his wishes. In more recent decades, the pope had received all the delegates themselves at the beginning of a congregation. At the Thirtieth Congregation in 1957, five years before Vatican II, Pope Pius XII had delivered an address that in great measure closed off any discussion of possible changes that the delegates might have wished to consider.[17] Pope Paul VI's talk was not similarly peremptory but it was serious.[18] He asked three questions: Where do you come from? Who are you? Where are you going? As a response to the first question, he recalled the origins of the Society—Ignatius, Manresa, the Spiritual Exercises, Rome, and Pope Paul III. To the second he replied that Jesuits were essentially religious, apostles, priests, united to the pope by a special vow. For the third he hoped, in the name of the Church, for a balanced adaptation that would meet current needs and be faithful to the essential characteristics of the Society, in accord with the charism of its founder, based on faith in a living Lord, at the service of the Church. The address concluded with the words "Let us walk together, free, obedient, united to each other in love of Christ for the greater glory of God."[19] The tensions of the juxtapositions of "apostle" and "priest" and of "free" and "obedient" were to surface all too quickly in the next weeks and months.

Day-to-day business began on December 4. One member from each assistancy was chosen for the Committee to Report on the State of the Society, and one from each assistancy for the Committee for Screening Postulata. The first of these groups was to gather information from individual delegates and from regional groups of delegates on the present strong and weak features of the Society, and to draw up a report thereon as a help to the congregation in its work. In times past, the committee had been charged simply with looking to impediments to the healthy functioning of the Society. The Thirty-first Congregation had broadened its scope to include a positive assessment as well. The second committee was to plunge into the ocean of postulata sent to the congregation. It had the responsibility of channeling them to specific committees that

---

[17] As one of the delegates remarked, the purpose of summoning a general congregation was to enable the Society to look at itself, to consider its present circumstances, and to chart its future. It was not supposed to gather simply so that before it ever began it could be told by the pope what to do. He had regular and ample enough ways of doing that should he so wish, and the Society would accede to his wishes; but a general congregation would be impeded in its very reason for existence if a pope were to preempt its deliberations.

[18] GC 32, Document I, Address of Pope Paul VI, Dec. 3, 1974, pp. 519–36.

[19] Ibid., p. 536.

would draw up and discuss and propose legislation on those subjects most important for the Society's future, in the light of their particular postulata and of the report on the state of the Society.

All was not work. Little was play. Much was prayer. At the end of each of three days (December 4, 5, and 6), the General gave a talk to all the delegates for their personal reflection. The successive themes were the challenge of the world and the mission of the Society, the guidance of the Holy Spirit, and God alone as our hope.

Inside the congregation the work went on. The Commission on the State of the Society elected as chairman Vincent O'Keefe of the New York Province. He was one of the general assistants and had been several times, in the absence of Fr. Arrupe, temporary vicar general. The Commission on Postulata elected as chairman Carlo Martini, rector of the Pontifical Biblical Institute[20]

A new body functioned at this meeting too. By previous law the general had always presided at meetings of the congregation. But the Thirty-first Congregation had set up a "council of the presidency" to help the General in preparing the meetings and to relieve him, through several of its members, of the burden of presiding day after day at those plenary sessions. The council comprised the general secretary (Johannes Gerhartz), a member from each of the two committees mentioned above (Jean-Yves Calvez and Cecil McGarry, provincial of Ireland), two members chosen by the General (Robert Mitchell from New York, president of the Jesuit Conference of the Provincials of the United States, and Roberto Tucci from Naples, former editor of *Civiltà Cattolica* and currently director of the Vatican Radio).

Discussions on the state of the Society got under way, carried out especially in small groups of members set up along language lines. Out of such groups began to emerge also some feeling for the priorities which the congregation ought to address. Additions to the procedural formula had mandated an early decision by the congregation on a list of priority topics to be treated in such manner that no other topics would be brought up for formal consideration by the congregation as a whole without a new and explicit decision to do so.

Outside the congregation, the press began its search for the unusual. The Pope's address to the delegates drew headlines. Too often the headlines were more attention-attracting than accurate; for example, in two German papers, "Pope Warns Jesuits"; in the *London Times,* "Pope Warns Questioning Jesuits"; in the *Guardian,* "Pope's Harsh Words for Jesuits"; and in the Italian *Messaggero,* "The Pope to the Jesuits: Why Do You Doubt?" Most of this genuinely puzzled or dismayed the delegates. More of such simplistic views were

---

[20] A little later Fr. Martini became rector of the Gregorian University, and he is now the Cardinal Archbishop of Milan.

to come later on during the congregation. In fairness to the newspapers, it must be said that the articles themselves were usually more nuanced than the headlines.[21]

Priorities

The linguistic groups mentioned earlier had been discussing not only the state of the Society but also priorities among the hundreds of postulata. Fortunately they had not had to start from scratch with those postulata. The preparatory committee had been at work two weeks before the congregation even began. Made up of five already elected delegates (from India, the United States, Italy, Ireland, and Chile), it had put together a list of forty-eight headings as a summary of the topics treated in the postulata. Having this list in hand saved the Commission on Postulata some time. Toward the end of its major work, the Commission on Postulata presented to the whole congregation a list of eight principal topics that had emerged from the language-group discussions. And finally, after several plenary sessions on the matter, the whole congregation, in the relatively short time of ten days after the meeting had begun, on December 12 approved by vote a list of six subjects to which it wanted to give priority. This was a very important step, for it helped to define from now on, in a variety of configurations, most of the major concerns of the congregation. The topics, each of which received more than an absolute majority of the votes of the congregation, were (1) criteria for Jesuit apostolates, (2) "mission" and obedience, (3) poverty in its institutional and juridical aspects, (4) the promotion of justice, (5) the fourth vow, and (6) formed members, grades, and the question of types of membership in the Society.

Somewhat earlier, the congregation had given the General and the Commission on Postulata the authority to decide which specific working committees were needed to handle the topics to be dealt with. So on the same afternoon of the vote on the six priorities mentioned above, the General announced his decision to set up ten such working committees. Six of the committees were to deal with those priorities; four others were to deal with subjects that the previous congregation had mandated or that were clearly of substantial concern to a good number of present delegates. The four additional committees were (7) on formation of Jesuits, (8) on spiritual and community life and union in the Society, (9) on governance and congregations, and (10) on last vows or final incorporation into the Society. Lastly, two somewhat technical

---

[21] The prize for imagination-run-riot went—for the time being—to a hilarious account in a Flemish-Dutch newspaper which said that among the subjects of discussion for the congregation would be the resignation of the Pope, and that if Paul VI did resign, the Jesuit General, Fr. Arrupe, could be expected to put forward his candidacy for the papacy, even if only to set a precedent!

committees were set up. The first, on juridical matters, was composed largely of canonist members of the congregation; the other was to deal with procedural matters in the conduct of the meetings day by day.

Now the congregation could get down to work—almost. One last problem intervened. Some delegates wanted to establish a "priority of priorities." This led to some confusion—procedural, linguistic, substantive, and a mix of all three. Was it enough simply to have from the start a list of items that the congregation thought it good to deal with? Was a vote on the set of topics meant to be a listing in the order of rank? Would it not be good to have some time for a general discussion toward choosing a topic that would provide a "horizon" for all of the subsequent work of the congregation, and a priority to guide all of its discussion and debate and decree drafting and legislating?

The discussion both at this point and later made the matter yet more complicated. Some could hardly fail to note that "horizon" and "priority" were surely not the same thing, as one American later remarked perceptively. He said that if they were to be taken synonymously, then a "priority of priorities" would become a "horizon of all horizons," an absolute totality, and the congregation would effectively have to deal with everything, temporal and eternal, material and spiritual. In any case, the delegates voted to spend several days in group discussions on what emerged as a joint theme from this preliminary proposal for a priority of priorities. The two subjects of discussion were to be the criteria for the apostolates of the Society today and the promotion of justice in the world.

These group discussions were meant to have a twofold result: They were to deepen the understanding of these topics in their specific commissions, and they were to lead to a growth in the knowledge of one another on the part of the members of the congregation. From all of this discussion would come, ideally and consequently, a growing awareness of the "style" which the congregation might wish to adopt. These were all worthy objectives, but the conjunction of them all did not help toward clarity in understanding them. The introduction of the promotion of justice as seemingly a criterion of equal or greater importance than any other ones, still unspecified, was disquieting to some participants. But the congregation nonetheless settled down to this work seriously and with basic internal serenity, and over the weekend of December 14–15 the assignment of members to all the commissions took place.[22]

---

[22] In addition, during the course of the congregation, several other groups or ad hoc committees were set up. They dealt, for example, with the educational apostolate, the Roman institutions of higher education entrusted to the Society, chastity, inculturation, and implementation of the congregation. Most of the groups gave reports to the whole congregation. Only the one on inculturation actually became the basis for a decree of the congregation. The work on the Roman houses went to the General and to a special meeting of provincials; the work on chastity, done in cooperation with the commission on formation, went to the

Uncertainties—The Pope and the Congregation

On Monday, December 16, the serenity was broken. That morning Fr. Arrupe informed the plenary session that he had received a letter from Cardinal Villot, the papal Secretary of State, delivered on behalf of the Holy See and dated December 3, the same day as the papal address to the delegates.[23] The letter dealt with the fourth vow taken by professed members of the Society. To understand its context one has to review briefly some earlier relations of the Pope and the Society leading up to the congregation. As mentioned previously, in 1972 Fr. Arrupe had told Pope Paul VI of the preparations for a congregation as soon as they had begun. On November 21, 1974, about ten days before the congregation started, he had visited the Pope and given him a copy of the volume containing all the postulata. He also noted in a memorandum the topics with which he thought the congregation would in all likelihood deal, given the postulata and the tenor of the preparatory period for the congregation. Among those topics, the General had noted for the Pope the possibility that the congregation might want to request a change in the Institute of the Society so that nonpriests could also take the fourth vow.

In his address to the delegates on December 3, the Pope urged the desirability of renewal in the Society and the changes necessary to bring this about, and talked about the "double charism of the apostle . . . fidelity—not sterile and static, but living and fruitful . . . and service to all men, our brethren traveling with us towards the future."[24] This might well have encouraged in the delegates an optimistic spirit toward adaptation, especially when coupled with the concluding words of that address, previously quoted here: "Let us walk together, free, obedient, united to each other in the love of Christ."[25] At the same time, however, the Pope had also said something in that same address that was to come to the fore later in the congregation:

> We are certainly aware that if obedience demands much from those who obey, it demands even more of those who exercise authority. The latter are required to listen without partiality to the voices of all their sons, to surround themselves with prudent counsellors in order to evaluate situations sincerely, to choose before God what best corresponds to his will and to intervene with firmness whenever there is departure from that will.[26]

General.

[23] GC 32, Document II, Letter of the Cardinal Secretary of State to Father General, Dec. 3, 1974, pp. 537–38.

[24] GC 32, Document I, p. 532.

[25] Ibid., p. 536.

[26] Ibid., p. 535.

Undoubtedly the Pope had such a right and responsibility, and he had no obligation whatsoever to disclose who it was from whom he took advice. But as the congregation progressed, it was never clear to its members which "sons" of the Society, other than the ones chosen by their own brethren for the congregation, he was listening to in his evaluation of the actions of the congregation, nor which "counsellors" outside—or inside—the Society he was relying on for prudent advice. This situation was to help create a growing sense of uncertainty about how well the intentions and actions of the congregation were interpreted and understood.

To turn from the context to the letter itself, the secretary of state noted that the Pope had "indicated his lively concern . . . that the Society itself, in its praiseworthy and responsible attempt at 'aggiornamento' in accord with the needs of the times, would remain faithful in its essential characteristics set down in the fundamental rule of the Order, that is, in the Formula of the Institute."[27] He then said that the Pope had not failed to consider the possibility that a proposal might be advanced to extend to all the members of the Society the fourth vow of special obedience to the Supreme Pontiff "with regard to missions." The next phrases of the letter were the crucial ones, in themselves and in further discussions in the congregation. "The Supreme Pontiff . . . desires to let you know that such a change in the light of more careful examination seems to present grave difficulties which would impede the approval necessary on the part of the Holy See."[28] The cardinal concluded by saying that he was sending the letter so that the General might have it before him "as the work of the General Congregation develops."

The first development, then, was for the congregation to ascertain what this meant for its work. On the one hand, the congregation had a mandate at hand from the Society itself, which it could hardly ignore. There were sixty-five official postulata from province congregations around the world asking for consideration of the the question of grades; forty-one of those postulata called for the abolition of the distinction in grades. On the other hand, there was the present letter saying that extension of the fourth vow seemed to present grave difficulties that would impede the necessary approval on the part of the Holy

---

[27] GC 32, Document II, p. 537.

[28] Ibid., pp. 537–38. The original Italian of the sentence and its Latin translation are as follows: "A questo proposito, il Sommo Pontefice desidera che Le sia communicato che tale innovazione, ad un attento esame, sembra presentare gravi difficoltà, che impedirebbero la necessaria approvazione da parte della Santa Sede." "In hunc finem, Summus Pontifex desiderat ut tecum communicetur talem innovationem, sub luce accurati examinis, videri graves difficultates præsentare, quæ necessariam ex parte Sanctæ Sedis approbationen impedirent." See Decreta C.G. XXXII (Rome: Curia S. I., 1975), 178f., for full texts of both versions. The letter was immediately translated into the several vernacular languages used by the congregation itself.

See. It was clear that these several matters, namely, consideration of grades, abolition of the distinction in grades, and extension of the fourth vow, were not exactly the same things. It was also clear that they were intimately linked. It was not at all clear which of these matters fell under the ban imposed by this letter, or whether the whole question was excluded from treatment. In discussion, some of the congregation members said that the letter absolutely prohibited any further treatment at all. In part they relied on their understanding of Vatican language and style of expression. Others said that it was surely a caution, but that the letter itself used conditional or tentative terms such as "seems" or "would impede."[29] For this second group of delegates, there were clear and obvious terms to use if the Holy See had wished to forbid any further treatment, and the Holy See deliberately had not used them. In the long run, the first opinion was to prove correct; for the congregation learned later that the letter had intended to prohibit any further action. From the letter itself, it always remained ambiguous whether the Holy See intended to preclude dealing with all three of the parts noted above, namely, consideration of grades, abolition of the distinction in grades, and extension of the fourth vow, or only one or some combination of the three parts. For the moment, however, the congregation, faced with a green light from the Society and what it saw as an amber light from the Holy See, proceeded with caution. Later it learned that the Vatican light had been red.

A "Priority of Priorities"?

Other matters went forward. The most immediate one was the "priority of priorities." Seventeen linguistic groups and the twelve assistancy groups had studied the topic and had forwarded more than fifty pages of material from those discussions to two of the working commissions, those on Apostolates (I) and on Justice (IV). The two commissions now presented a general combined report to the entire congregation, after which plenary discussion took place. Two preoccupations were noted in the report and underlay that discussion, as they had also conditioned the smaller-group deliberations. They were not necessarily antitheses but rather emphases. The one preoccupation was that the congregation take seriously and highlight the connection between the message of the Gospel and concern for the oppressed; the other was that the congregation take seriously and highlight the specifically spiritual character of the work of the Society. The large number of postulata on justice as a primary concern of the Society's apostolates was cited as a reason for forward movement. Ambiguity about the meaning of justice and the implication that the Society was

---

[29] The Italian *sembra* and *impedirebbero* and the Latin *videri* and *impedirent* gave this indication.

presuming to take on the role of the Church itself were urged as reasons for going slow.

Some thirty-five delegates spoke during several days of discussion. Gradually it became clear that a central point around which differences revolved was how to put together at the same time a priority commitment to the promotion of justice with commitments to several other central tasks, such as the commission given by Pope Paul VI to deal with atheism, the concern for evangelization, and the responsibility for preserving the fundamental character of the Society. Some who wanted "justice" as a "horizon" or priority commitment noted that the Society quite naturally assumed that "learning" was already such a priority in all of its work, and asked why justice could not equally be so. With a somewhat rhetorical flourish, one of the delegates asked which was closer to the Gospel, a commitment to learning or a commitment to justice.

After all others had spoken, Fr. General expressed his own reflections on an option for justice. He spoke briefly but eloquently. He thought that such a work was inescapable, that it came from the Gospel itself, that it flowed from the priestly character of the Society, that Ignatius was several centuries ahead of his time in understanding what priestly ministry was, that justice, as the Gospel envisaged it, had to be preached through the cross, and that if the Society took on this work, the cross would quickly be present. With a foresight which has been confirmed in the years since the congregation, he said that "despite our prudence and fidelity to our priesthood and religious charism," we would find that those who do injustice and who might often be among the benefactors or friends or relatives of Jesuits would "accuse us of Marxism or subversion, and will withdraw their friendship from us and, consequently, their previous trust and economic support." Is the congregation ready, he asked, "to enter on the sterner way of the cross, that which will bring us misunderstanding from civil and ecclesiastical authorities and our best friends?"[30] At the end of all the discussion, the chairmen of the working committees assured the delegates that they would review their original report and all the comments from the floor as they worked on a draft proposal for enactment by the congregation.

Several weeks of the congregation had now elapsed. Much of the humdrum work of getting down to the details of all the subjects to be considered was well under way. But the attention getter had been the discussion on the promotion of justice. That discussion became part, too, of the background against which the Pope was assessing the congregation. For whatever reasons and with whatever advice, both still unknown, this question of justice was for him linked with the question of grades. The way the congregation was dealing with both subjects the Pope could view as likely to lead to the diminution of

---

[30] GC 32, Session of Dec. 20, 1974, as reported in *News: General Congregation 32*, Dec. 20, 1974.

the primarily sacerdotal nature of the Society, the weakening of priestly ministry, and an undue political and social emphasis in Jesuit ministries. As a matter of fact, there was no such inclination at all among the delegates to be other than a priestly order. But what happened later in the congregation on the question of grades (as will be recounted here) served only to reinforce in him that original impression.

Day by Day—and Its Implications

The big news and the sense of important activity came from the plenary sessions of the congregation. The utterly necessary work went on in the context of a daily schedule at the level of the working commissions and their subcommittees and their yet further subdivisions. That day-to-day schedule went somewhat as follows. Mornings from nine to noon were very often occupied, after the first two weeks or so, with commission sessions, language-group meetings, or subcommittee meetings. Only when draft documents had gone through all previous steps was there a plenary session to deal with them. When there were no plenary or particular meetings, most of the delegates were busy reading the new material that on a daily basis filled their mail boxes, or they were busy contributing to that flood through the reports, drafts, and revisions which they themselves were commissioned to write.[31]

Meetings, plenary or otherwise, ended at noon and resumed at four in the afternoon. In the intervening hours, the celebration of the Eucharist came first, sometimes by language groups, sometimes in the several houses where the delegates lived. There were earlier Masses, too, and regular prayer sessions, even before the meetings began in the morning. On special occasions all the delegates would gather for Mass in the chapel of the curia. The main meal of the day, dinner, was usually taken about one o'clock, followed by common recreation. The early afternoon left time to rest, to catch up with reading (which was a never ending task), and to get what exercise one could by a walk. (Joggers were not known to be common among the delegates.) From four to seven the round of meetings went on again. Supper was available after that. Then the delegates went back to their lodgings, there to reflect on, or wonder about, or record, or be weary of, or be happy about the events of the day and to work on the material for the morrow.

The curia had limited space and could provide lodging for only some of the delegates. Most of them had to live in religious houses that were run especially during summer months as pilgrim hostels or *pensioni*. Some delegates were assigned to a rather nondescript hotel a block from the curia. Each lodging

---

[31] By the end of the congregation all of the delegates had received at least two thousand pages of material, not including the dozens or hundreds of further pages that each individual delegate received from his particular commission.

had its advantages, each its temptations to laughter or fury. At the religious *pensioni*, the nuns were very solicitous to provide for the delegates but, understandably, on their own terms.[32] At the curia the accommodations were convenient and the community was very welcoming, but one never escaped the atmosphere of the congregation. At the hotel, one got away from the congregation but had little incentive to stay in dimly lit, cold, dull, blue gray rooms, which became even colder after the boiler blew up in early January.

Saturday afternoons and all day Sundays were free. The only other times off were Christmas Day and New Year's Day and one-half day on each of their eves, and one day in January, about halfway through the three months of the congregation.

Rome itself in all its beauty, diversity, and grandeur was for some a matchless attraction. How they enjoyed it varied with the delegates. As pilgrim or tourist or historian or lover of art and architecture, one could visit churches (more of them than one could ever get to) or tramp through museums (some were always closed "for restoration," at least in part). Sunday mornings brought a watchful wait at St. Peter's Square for the famous papal blessing at noon (and improbably but regularly one would meet in the assembled throng of thousands a person he knew). There were opportunities to sip coffee at the sidewalk outside a *trattoria* while observing the crowds at the holiday booths on the Piazza Navona, to walk in the Pincio gardens and watch the sun turn to gold the baroque domes of papal Rome, to inspect the flea market on a Sunday morning and perhaps make a small purchase where the bargains were interesting, but less so than the people. Most evocative of the complexities of Rome were visits, guidebook in hand, to the republican, imperial, papal, and modern monuments, squares, palaces, temples, and streets of a city in which everything spoke of a grandeur or a crime, a folly or a virtue, all of which helped some of the delegates to put the congregation in perspective.

As the days became the weeks which became the months, the members of the congregation needed that perspective, for several reasons. The work was demanding and important and always there. The uncertainty and misunderstandings in the relationship with the Pope were psychologically and spiritually enervating. Perhaps most important, and perhaps true of the history of any general congregation, the delegates were involved in an enterprise for which most of them were largely unprepared by temperament, background, or experience. Members of the Society of Jesus have usually turned from very active apostolic work and become delegates to the congregation, where they had to

---

[32] At one of those houses, no delegate could ever get a key to the building from the mother superior. Instead, they were told, a sister would wait at the door for them, no matter at what hour they came in. One of the delegates was tempted on the feast of St. Peter publicly to petition the Saint in the collect prayer for one of his keys.

spend their time over documents and discussions. They have individually had little taste for politics; in fact, at times they have refused to recognize the obvious existence of this aspect of life. But inevitably there have been for the internal and external life of the Church political implications to any action of a general congregation. Lastly, because the Society of Jesus, for its own good reasons, does not have a capitular form of government for its ordinary, ongoing lawmaking, many of its members have had almost no experience of legislative processes or of parliamentary practice; hence, in any congregation such delegates become acquainted with all of this in a very short time.

The average period of time between general congregations has been eleven years. Very many, if not the majority, of the members have been elected for the first time as delegates. Therefore, there has been no ongoing, uninterrupted tradition of a lawmaking body whereby experienced members smoothly induct new hands into that tradition. The Society of Jesus has opted not to have continuing or regularly scheduled legislative meetings. The delegates to any general congregation then necessarily have had to bear the consequences outlined above. If a given congregation was brief, its members did not experience those consequences so vividly. If a congregation comprised a large number of delegates, some of whom had little experience and less interest in procedure, and was confronted with complicated matters requiring extended debate, its members could not fail to notice those consequences. If, as in the Thirty-second and some previous congregations, there was the added complication of misunderstanding or disagreement with some offices of the Holy See, then those consequences became aggravatedly painful.

Step by Step

The day-by-day life of the congregation was yet further divided by the step-by-step procedures through which material moved from being an idea conceived in the mind of the Jesuit who wrote the postulatum in the most remote province of the Society to a finished document adopted by the congregation as part of the Society's official legislation. Everything started with such a postulatum or proposal or request for action by the congregation. That postulatum went to the appropriate working commission. To take but one example, which we shall continue to use for the purposes of this section of the study, the Commission on Governance had twenty-two members from twenty-two different provinces. Of course, very soon the members of the commission had to choose a chairman. The next two steps were to read and analyze all the postulata on the subject at hand and to decide how best the commission could begin to deal with them. Almost always the best approach was to appoint subcommissions to consider particular parts of the overall topic represented in the postulata. Thus, for example, the Commission on Governance recognized quickly that the two main divisions for the numerous postulata were the ordinary governance of the Society, which goes on regularly through the general and provincial offices, and the extraordinary governance of the several congregations or special meetings, namely, the congregation of the province, of provincials, and of procurators, and the general congregation. A subcommission took shape for each of those two main divisions, with members appointed from the whole group according to interests, backgrounds, and expertise.

As happens in the life cycle of a cell, a subcommission often further subdivided in order to deal with particular topics. The group which was to deal with congregations became two further groups: one for general congregations, the other for all the other such extraordinary means of governance. The other working commissions similarly separated into smaller units according to the subjects to be treated. The members of each specific small working group then reviewed the postulata particular to its concerns, talked informally among themselves about their reactions to the proposals, and tested with each other their personal, tentative responses to the questions raised and their possible solutions to the problems posed. When some glimmers of clarity and agreement appeared concerning a proposal for a particular point, one of the subcommittee members was deputed to write a draft of it. Meanwhile, of course, the same process was going on in all ten commissions and their smaller subcommissions and yet smaller working groups.

When a small working group had reviewed and accepted a proposal, it went to a meeting of the subcommission. For example, the group dealing with general congregations considered several versions of a proposal on the size, composition, and duration of a general congregation. The members of the subcommission on congregations individually reviewed it, met together to discuss and debate it, and made evident to the working group what it could and could not accept. The group prepared a new version on the basis of those reactions and brought it back to the subcommission. After further debate and amendment, that body approved the proposal for discussion and debate in the whole commission. The same process took place there, with the necessity— sometimes a benefit, often an obstacle—of considering how this particular proposal fitted as a part into the whole decree which was being fashioned out of many such parts.

The example cited here involved an uncontroversial and relatively uncomplicated issue. For the commissions that dealt with controversial and complicated topics, the process was the same; but to carry it out was fraught with far more difficulties, requiring clarity, patience, honesty, openness, conviction, and the willingness recommended by St. Ignatius, to "suppose that every good Christian is more ready to put a good interpretation on another's statement than to condemn it as false."[33]

---

[33] *Spiritual Exercises*, [22].

The usefulness of straw votes was obvious in such circumstances. Without at all committing the congregation to a particular position, such votes helped the commissions to use their time and talents and energies to the best effect. Such straw votes indicated the general lines of solutions to problems and answers to questions and responses to opportunities that might be most likely to gain the assent of the congregation when in full assembly it formally voted on a proposal.

Such a definitive vote, of course, was the goal to which all of this detailed work was aimed. After a commission had approved a first draft or preliminary proposal, the secretary of the congregation arranged for its distribution to all the members of the congregation. All were invited to make written comments for the benefit of the commission. Depending on those comments, the commission might even at this stage meet again and amend the preliminary draft. In any case, those comments helped the *relator* or, to use current legislative terms, the "floor manager of a bill," to prepare his remarks as he introduced a second draft of the proposal in the assembly hall before the whole membership of the congregation. After he had done that, the small language groups met to discuss the proposal, usually for a half or full day.

" . . . That the Truth Might Appear"

Then the debate began in plenary session. It might have been as brief as half a day; it might have stretched over several days. Each member had the right to speak on every proposal. Some exercised the right to a great extent. Fortunately, others were more restrained. If a delegate had made a written request to speak, he was permitted to speak for seven minutes; if, during the debate itself, he signaled his wish to speak, five minutes were his apportioned time. Neither period seemed long in itself. But when the electronic indicator board sparkled as green as a summer field, the delegates had only to multiply requests by minutes to know when to settle in for a long session. Or when, as one delegate remarked, "seven minutes is not even the beginning of the commencement of the start to an introduction to a speech," the others knew that neither buzzer nor bell from the presiding officer, but only a personal sense of restraint, would dam the flow of oratory.

When a topic of great importance or delicacy was the subject for plenary discussion, the air of seriousness in the *aula* was palpable. Almost always the discussion was both frank and respectful, but tensions could and did arise, as was only to be expected, especially as the congregation dragged on and as the uncertainties of the relations with the Holy See weighed down upon the members.

When discussion of a text had been completed, it went back to its commission for revision in accord with any formal amendments or the general tenor of the debate. Once in a while, earlier or at this point, a special drafting committee would be set up and charged with refashioning a difficult text and putting it into final shape to correspond to the mind of the congregation, as revealed in the debates. This was not a task to be envied; it often involved long meetings, late nights, close deadlines, great energy, frayed nerves, and organizational and writing skills of a high order. Then, some time later, after a week or ten days or more, back again to the full assembly came the definitive draft. Debate again might well ensue. An interval of at least one day followed after close of debate. Then, at last, a final vote took place. On persons, votes were secret; on documents, they were public. Section by section, sometimes paragraph by paragraph, the delegates voted on the proposal at hand. Tedious though this procedure might have been, it left no doubt in the minds of the delegates what precisely it was that they were accepting or rejecting. Each delegate contributed to the Christmas-tree effect of the indicator board high up behind the General's presiding table, as the red (for "non placet") and the green (for "placet") lights snapped on. At the end of such detailed voting, a final ballot was taken on the proposal as a whole. When the subject in question had been complicated, ardently debated, and of great importance, the sense of accomplishment was audible.

And then, waiting in the wings, often after having gone through all the procedures here detailed at too great a length, was the next document to come to the floor.

The State of the Society

At the very beginning of the congregation in early December, the Commission on the State of the Society had started its work. At the end of December it submitted its report to all the delegates. While its members were simultaneously serving on other working commissions, they had also taken on the complications of preparing this report. Individual delegates and seventeen small language groups and the twelve assistancy groups had submitted their own observations on the state of the Society. At the decision of the General, the assistancy meetings early in the congregation on the state of the Society had even had the opportunity to hear in some detail and with complete candor complaints about the Society and its members which various people had conveyed to the Holy See and with which the Vatican had taxed the General. The commission itself had received from the General specific documents on that subject. The members of the congregation were not surprised at reports of both abuses and plain and simple foolishness on the part of specific Jesuits. Given original sin, such failings were, regrettably, to be expected. Many delegates were distressed, however, at the way in which specific examples had been generalized and particular instances had been reported to the Holy See that, on the basis of their personal and direct knowledge, they knew had not taken place as depicted.[34] Nonetheless, they did take seriously all of this information because it obviously influenced the negative way in which the Holy See sometimes saw the Society, even when the Holy See itself emphasized at the beginning of one of its documents that most Jesuits were serious religious who lived out loyally their obligations and engaged in apostolates of great value and service to the Church.

After considering this and much other material, the commissions wrote a provisional report and asked for written comments on it from the delegates individually or gathered in assistancy groups. Those comments formed the substance of another report to the delegates. The commission members identified what each of them saw as the most significant negative and positive elements about the state of the Society. Item by item, the commission voted on a synthesis of all this material, and those items that were accepted by majority vote became the basis of the definitive report which went to all the delegates on December 31.

That report began by noting the overwhelming climate of change prevailing in the world, the Church, and the Society in the years since Vatican II, the differences in problems and solutions from region to region, the difficulty of judging as positive or negative the elements that were still in flux, and the confidence in the Lord, the Church, and the Society that ought to undergird any judgment about where God was working among Jesuits and about where they interposed obstacles to his work in the life and activity of the Society. The report was structured in several broad categories: adaptations and renewal and their effect on Jesuit spirit and identity, the apostolic life and activities of the Society, the personal life of Jesuits, the community life of the Society, formation of younger Jesuits, and the government of the Society.[35]

This report formed the basis of discussion in a plenary session on January 2, at which the chairman of the commission responded to questions and elaborated on particular items for the many delegates who wished to comment on the report.

After that discussion, the General, against a background of his nine years in office, presented his own impression of the state of the Society and his

---

[34] One delegate, after hearing many of the institutions of his province—with the exception of the one to which he belonged—wrongly indicted for one aberration or another, wondered wryly whether his community and apostolate were doing anything at all.

[35] "On the one hand" alternated with "on the other" in an obvious regularity in the report. If the report thus saw both sides of a situation, it was because, in its estimation, such was the reality. Anathemata and accolades are impressive when they stand alone. They do, however, in that case have the obvious inconvenience of falsity.

view of the state of relationships between the Jesuit curia and the Holy See and its Vatican offices. Among the central points of a very frank and warmly personal talk were the following. He saw as a "common denominator for understanding the current situation . . . the need for [the] Society to undertake a true apostolic adaptation to the new conditions of the contemporary world, conditions that find themselves in constant change."[36] For change to be helpful, he judged necessary "(1) an acute sense of discernment and internal freedom; (2) a certain maturity, both spiritual and human; (3) a humble and apostolic desire to learn new things." He thought the Society was a basically healthy body, at times undergoing a variety of tests that occasionally may have fatigued it. Continuing the analogy of a body, Fr. General suggested that this fatigue could have come over the Society because of tasks for which it was unprepared, or because of a functional disorder as it attempted to assimilate elements abnormal in type or quantity, or because of a reaction that rejects harmful elements. In the Society there was "movement of spirits" on vital subjects, such as contemporary faith, union of minds and hearts, the apostolate, faithfulness to the hierarchical Church, and poverty. These he regarded as basically positive and potentially productive of much good.

To one defect the General called specific attention. It was "a lack of fidelity toward the Society among [Jesuits] who . . . see themselves as not a part of it, but rather judge it from outside and seem to reserve to themselves the right to accept or reject what the Society, through its superiors, or even through a general congregation, has decided to decree, and to pass judgment, even publicly and in harsh language and with bitterness, on what others do."[37] He spoke too of formation, departure from the Society, spiritual governance, participation and responsibility and discernment, creativity in novel circumstances, and the importance of encouraging the development and growth of the positive elements in the Society rather than simply concentrating on the elimination of the negative. He thought it necessary for the governing of the Society that the congregation set forth, even if only quite briefly, some definite principles and some clear practical norms that would serve as a basis for a man's truly belonging to the Society. The General asked the delegates to give him such clearly stated and concrete programs so that he could implement its decrees.

In emphasizing the need to accept sincerely the decrees of the general congregation as essential to union and charity in the Society, he made a somewhat surprising comment. "It will be impossible to allow to happen again what happened in recent years, namely, that some regarded the Thirty-first General Congregation as something of a deviation from the spirit of St. Ignatius, that

---

[36] *News: General Congregation 32,* January 8, 1975.

[37] Ibid.

they should have revealed this publicly and not infrequently in the unsuitable form of anonymous letters. If this were to happen again, it would render the government of the Society impossible."[38]

Relations with the Holy See came up explicitly because a request had been made that the General speak to the whole congregation on the subject. His remarks followed immediately after those on the state of the Society. Delegates clearly had been perturbed by rumors at home or in Rome about the state of those relations.[39] The General said that his abiding purpose had been to achieve "great simplicity, reverence, and fidelity" in such contacts. He first spoke of his relations with the Holy Father, making it evident how genuinely he esteemed Pope Paul VI. He affirmed that he was not aware of any notable differences in matters of judgment between himself and the Pope, but if they existed he would gladly change. He assured the delegates that the Pope, in turn, truly loved and esteemed the Society and understood the difficulties of governance even when he was distressed by the faults of Jesuits, especially thoughtless and public criticism. Doctrinal questions, whether propounded in classroom or journal, were a special preoccupation and concern of the Pope. As to the offices of the Roman curia, there too the General thought that relationships in general were good, even if in particular cases difficulties existed arising out of doctrinal or disciplinary affairs and the way to handle them. He thought that the Society had suffered great harm from the rumors in recent years about supposed mistrust in the relations of the Holy See and the Society, and he declared that certain Jesuits could not consider themselves without blame for such rumors. Current means of gathering the information that would present a complete, documented, and reasonably objective picture of the reality of the Society were, in his judgment, inadequate. Hence partial, or even strongly negative, images of the Society may have developed in some of the Vatican congregations. He concluded by stating that even with the mistakes which inevitably arise from the difficult problems of change and adaptation, if collaboration with the Holy See and the Pope was positive and generous, then such faults did not mean that the Society was unfaithful in its vocation to serve the Church.[40]

---

[38] Ibid.

[39] In Rome, where everything means something, it had not passed without notice that after two hundred years of almost total obscurity, Clement XIV, the pope who suppressed the Society, was the subject of a laudatory article in *Osservatore Romano* on December 3, 1974, the day of the address by the Pope to the delegates. The occasion for the article was the second centenary of Clement's death in 1774, but that anniversary had occurred some months before, in July. The article even noted that "some, it is even said, have received divine graces and temporal favors through his intercession."

[40] Subsequent events, in the immediate future of the congregation and now in the immediate past of the Society, make clear that the General's assessment of the state of relationships was far too optimistic.

Questions followed. In a quite unprecedented move, the General opened himself to any and all queries from the delegates about what he had said. At first only a few lights on the voting board flashed rather hesitantly to indicate the wish to speak. When Fr. Arrupe answered the first questions with complete frankness and simplicity, brightened by touches of humor, a blaze of lights went on. The questions ranged all the way from the sources of malicious rumors ("I think I ought to tell you that in private") to communal discernment, from departures from the Society to means to improve relations with the Holy See, from violations of secrecy to ways to keep the Society better informed of its fundamental soundness. Some postulata sent to Rome had asked for a vote of confidence in the General, and some delegates may have come to Rome wondering how well the years of Fr. Arrupe's generalate had gone. Hesitations might still have remained, but the vigorous and continuing applause at the end of that most unusual session was a more evident witness to the basic solidarity of the Society with the General than any such vote would have been.

Going in Circles

By the beginning of the second week in January, each of the ten working commissions had furnished its *relatio prævia*, or preliminary report. Soon the time was to come for the formal debate described earlier in this study. One would think it an occasion for a sigh of relief. It was not. Instead there were murmurings of apprehension. On January 10 the secretary published the results of a questionnaire on the progress of the congregation, given to the delegates several days earlier. Those results and worry about what seemed the increasingly cumbersome working procedures sparked on January 13 and 14 a debate, always vigorous, sometimes circular, once in a while obscure, rather inconclusive. It bore witness to a congregation temporarily confused.

The results of the questionnaire brought out what so far the delegates had found of positive value and of negative impact. Many thought very positive the Eucharistic concelebrations in or across relatively small language groups, the general atmosphere of kindness, patience, and humor, the behind-the-scenes staff work of the Jesuit curia, and the discussion sessions in the small-group or language or assistancy contexts. Problems were evident in the slow pace of the congregation, the constriction of working from postulata rather than from the basic questions underlying them, the overly large size of the commissions, the uncertainty of when a decision would be made about which topics were of such importance that they must really be concentrated on and which were of less importance and thus should be excluded from an overcrowded agenda, and the difficulty of communication and collaboration across commission lines. Most important and unsettling was the uncertainty about what to do and how to do it in the days ahead. The General had consulted about these matters with the chairmen of all the commissions and with the commission on screening postulata.

Especially important was the question of how to prepare documents in a form usable by the congregation without involving everyone in the congregation in a wearying and unprofitable marathon composition session. Two options were proposed. The congregation could continue its present procedure, which involved all the commission members working at the second and later drafts of the documents. Or the current commissions could be disbanded and small drafting committees of three or four members could be established to prepare those revised reports. These options may not have been clear enough in themselves or in the minds of the delegates. Whatever the reason, the debate went round in circles. The members of the congregation were caught in a dilemma. They realized that not everyone could be involved in writing every decree; at the same time they had a high sense of their individual and collective responsibility for the results of the congregation, and they were reluctant to commit that responsibility to small groups of three or four delegates.

The proposal adopted the next day resolved the dilemma. The full membership of each commission would choose from among its members an editorial or drafting team for the document to be presented. The entire commission would then give its judgment on the text eventually drafted, sending it back for revision if there were serious changes to be made, but not attempting to act as a group in writing the actual text. This decision set the course for the next several weeks. It imposed very heavy burdens on relatively few people, and it left some of the members feeling at loose ends with little to do at times but wait for material to come to them.

The "related questions" that some wished to address came next to the floor. They dealt mainly with the kind of documents that the congregation might wish to produce. Were they to be legal texts or mere declarations? Would they take into account regional differences and pluralism of viewpoints? When would it be best for the congregation to decide what the style and nature of a particular document should be? There were, of course, no ready answers until texts began to appear. Finally, several members pleaded, as a related question, for brevity in the documents; they sometimes did so in speeches which, by this time, seemed to lack that admirable quality.

At the end of this session, the General spoke about how he saw the interior state of the congregation so far. He judged that basically it was very positive. He spoke also about communal discernment as a need of the congregation; he saw such discernment as relatively successful so far in an informal manner, in smaller groups, and in liturgies, but practicable only with difficulty in a large group of 235 delegates. He then emphasized the freedom that the members had to gather in informal groups for prayer and discernment.

After these days of what seemed at first like circumambulation, the delegates were granted the next day, January 15, off for recreation. It joined Christmas and New Year's as the only three full days free in three months, other than Sundays.

Three of the commissions, those on the criteria and orientations of our apostolates, on mission and obedience, and on the promotion of justice, had already set to work on an experiment in collaboration. They gave to a small common group of their members the task of drafting a single text that would integrate the complementary concerns of the three commissions. Collaboration on the part of three different commissions accounted in part for the richness but also in part for the ambiguity of some of the material on faith and justice that the congregation would deal with in weeks to come.

Very quickly each commission chose its drafting committee or editorial team. At about the same time, the commission to screen postulata set up three special ad hoc committees to consider three topics that might come up for later discussion. They were on "the Roman houses" common to the whole Society, such as the Gregorian University or the Biblical Institute, on the apostolate of education, and on indigenization. Ultimately, the first two of these committees, after studying their subjects, did not propose specific decrees to the congregation. The third committee was to be most influential in producing the brief but cogent document on inculturation.

Straw Votes and Missed Signals

Straw Votes—Poverty

The commission on the legislation and practice of poverty in the Society provided on January 17 the first major occasion for the use of straw votes or ballots. Such votes, without yet committing the congregation, indicated the ways in which it was tending to view a particular matter. Before voting on a series of seventeen propositions that they had earlier received, the delegates in full assembly had the opportunity to hear from a chosen representative of each assistancy the reaction of the assistancy delegation as a whole to the proposals on poverty. Then the spokesman or *relator* for the commission itself answered in detail questions from the floor. Finally, he gave a clear, brief but comprehensive account of the history of the legislation of the Society on poverty and of the principles upon which the commission had relied as it prepared its proposals.

In twenty-two separate straw votes, with large majorities in all but one, the congregation accepted fourteen proposals, rejected three, and gave the commission a clear idea of its desires for the draft legislation. The congregation voted no to accepting permanently and without change the interim statutes of

1967 on poverty, to reviewing each of those interim statutes one by one, and to approving fixed revenues for Jesuit communities. It voted yes to the following proposals: general directives for a revision of the statutes on poverty; a distinction between community and apostolic work; the prohibition of turning to the profit of Jesuits, other than for an appropriate remuneration, any income or capital from such an apostolic work; the permission for the apostolic works of the Society to have resources, even revenue-producing ones; a clear definition of "fixed revenues"; permission for salaries for ministries unable to be undertaken gratuitously; permission for remuneration for stable ministries such as those of chaplain and teacher; the requirement that a community dispose of any annual surplus; a special province fund or participation in "social security" plans to provide for the sick and elderly; an organized procedure for disposal of a community's surplus; province sharing of resources by authority of major superiors; the establishment by the whole Society of a current-income apostolic and charitable fund for the benefit of needy communities or works; an annual community budget and balance sheet; and the recognition of the canonical ability of the provinces and of the Society as such to possess capital and income. As a matter of fact, with the appropriate specifications and nuances, these proposals became the bases for the actual legislation passed later in the congregation and then for the work after the congregation on the statutes written in conformity with that legislation. No wonder that at the end of the plenary session that day, the mood of the delegates was notably different from just a few days before. The fathers had a sense of real accomplishment and a mood of quiet euphoria was everywhere obvious.

Straw Votes—Grades

The next centrally important matter on which a working commission wanted further guidance from the congregation was the question of grades. This present account earlier mentioned the letter of December 3 from the secretary of state on behalf of the Holy See.[41] With what seemed to be the caution expressed in that letter clearly in their minds and with a sense of responsibility to the fifty-four out of eighty-five province congregations that had sent in official postulata on the matter, the members of the commission had done their work. Those postulata from all over the Society had made inescapable the obligation of the congregation at least to treat the matter of grades.

---

[41] It is interesting to note that all the direct communications with the Holy See on this present subject as well as on the congregation in general did not go through the Vatican Congregation for Religious, as in the usual course of events would be the case with matters dealing with religious orders, but rather through the Secretariat of State, the overall coordinating Vatican office with direct and regular, even daily, access to the Pope.

Commission VI, On Formed Members, gave the congregation a fifty-four-page *relatio prævia*, or preliminary report. It analyzed at length the postulata on the subject. It explored the implications of the Thirty-first Congregation's statement that the vocation of all Jesuits is a single vocation. Then it detailed the juridical meaning of each of the grades, especially in view of the Society as a clerical religious institute, and decided, at least for the sake of information, to sketch out all the options on grades that might be theoretically possible as they affected nonprofessed members of the Society with final vows, that is, the spiritual and temporal coadjutors. Those options ranged from the one extreme of simply abolishing the grade of spiritual coadjutor to the other extreme of making absolutely no change de jure or de facto in the current legislation. The commission had also asked the delegates for their tentative informal reactions to all the options and had provided a special form to be returned to the commission.

Now on January 20 the commission introduced its formal report. Because some of the material touched on pontifical law or on the fundamental characteristics of the institute of the Society, the congregation as a whole had to take a preliminary vote to ask whether it even wanted to discuss the material. That vote was overwhelmingly favorable to such a discussion. Then the delegates met in eighteen small linguistic groups to examine the specific proposals in the report. Finally, just before actual general discussion and debate took place on January 21 and 22, the congregation invited ten brothers, or temporal coadjutors, from ten different provinces to sit in on that discussion, and the General invited two of them, chosen by that group, to speak to the delegates in the general debate.

Fifty-seven speeches were given. There were several fundamental themes around which speakers circled; and each of those themes, depending on the delegate's point of view, could serve as a reason for or a reason against change in the Society's legislation on grades. The Ignatian or Jesuit charism was invoked. It demanded fidelity to what Ignatius had decided, or it stood for the openness to seek those changes that best put the Society at the service of Church and world. Justice and equality were called upon, either as values essentially social and psychological or as religious values of the Gospel and of Vatican II, but in both cases mandating changes in grades. The priestly character of the order was adduced. Some saw it as linked essentially to the fourth vow and grades and therefore forbidding change, a change that could even move the Society toward becoming a secular institute. Others were convinced that neither historically nor theologically was the priestly character necessarily linked to grades or the fourth vow. It should be clearly stated that no participant on either side of this aspect of the question exhibited the least desire to change that priestly character of the Society. The "mission" receivable from the pope was appealed to. Some said that only professed priests could be so summoned to such missions; others held that all Jesuits were capable of receiving those missions and, even if not by the fourth vow, were already bound to accept them. Several considerations dealt with the consequences of change or failure to change. Some said that dissatisfaction would be rife among Jesuits if something so fundamental was changed; others countered with the evidence of the enormous number of official requests from province congregations that change be undertaken. The need or desirability, or advantages or disadvantages, of taking up change regarding both the spiritual and the temporal coadjutors complicated the issue. Delay was suggested. Some saw delay as the prudent course; others saw it as a sign that the Society was incapable of renewing itself and of dealing with the obvious differences between theoretical structure and lived reality.

Obviously on the minds of all the delegates was the question, What was the mind of the Pope on the matter? Some were sure that it was already clear and, hence, the only appropriate response of the congregation was to drop the whole subject. Others still judged that the letter from the secretary of state had not foreclosed further consideration of the matter. A third group thought that even if that letter had meant to settle the subject in favor of no change and no discussion of it, still a twofold responsibility both urged and allowed a further pursuit of the issue. There was, first, the responsibility to the Society itself. But, more important, there was a responsibility to the Holy See. The congregation had to make sure that officially from the congregation itself, and not from any other unofficial source, no matter what it might be, the Holy See would hear the opinion of the congregation on what was obviously an urgent issue in the minds of Jesuits around the world. These delegates who wished to continue to deal with the matter said that the tradition and documents and past practice of the Society, of which they gave examples, made fully possible within the context of obedience a "representation" to the Pope. They urged this, in addition, because of an obvious inconsistency that confronted them. There were on the one hand the clear intentions of Vatican II's decree *Perfectæ Caritatis* (On the renewal of religious life), and later general declarations from the Holy See itself on the same matter; and there was on the other hand what was now presented as a particular intimation of the Pope's mind.

Finally, after all the wide-ranging and careful discussion and much prayer, the congregation took a series of indicative or straw votes on a variety of options. They were meant to indicate to the commission the direction in which the congregation wanted work to proceed in the drafting of a definitive text. That text would be presented to the whole assembly for its final discussion, emendation, rejection, or approval. The first question on which a straw vote was taken inquired whether it was the will of the congregation, in the light of the reasons presented and the very nature of the matter under discussion, to abolish grades in such wise that all formed Jesuits would be able to pronounce the same four vows without changing the sacerdotal character of the Society.

The second question asked whether it was the will of the congregation so to act even while taking into account the divergent views presented and the circumstances noted in the letter from the secretary of state. The third question asked whether it was the will of the congregation that a "representation" of the mind of the congregation should be made to the Pope. By a majority so very large that it surprised even the advocates of change, these votes indicated that the delegates were presently inclined to favor simply abolishing grades in the Society. On each of these questions, the vote was more than two-thirds affirmative. This produced a strong effect. As one of the minority was reported to have said privately, "This vote has made me think, far more than all the previous arguments. I shall have to rethink all my ways of looking at things."

Abolition of grades, of course, was not the only option, so further straw votes followed on other possibilities. Even if grades were to continue to exist, very heavy or strong majorities favored these further possibilities: removing the present conditionality of the coadjutors' vows, taking steps to increase coadjutor participation in province congregations and possibly in general congregations, eliminating distinctions between professed and spiritual coadjutors, and revising the criteria for profession of four vows. However, lesser but still large majorities showed a willingness, with grades still existent, to abolish the one grade of spiritual coadjutor, and also showed willingness at least to abolish the grade of spiritual coadjutor and to permit both groups of coadjutors to take three solemn vows. A proposal to have all members become formed coadjutors first, with some of them taking solemn vows later on, lost. And finally, down to defeat by an overwhelming margin went the proposal that the present congregation do nothing at all about grades.

Again, with a certain sense of quiet euphoria the session concluded. Nothing was decided, but at least and at last all had some sense of where a very great part of the congregation stood at present on a most urgent question. Everyone recognized the seriousness of the straw votes in themselves for the further work of the congregation and in the context of the unresolved uncertainties about the position of the Holy See. The regular procedure of the congregation to keep the Pope informed of its actions was, therefore, especially important on this occasion. Carlo Martini, the delegate who had officially been deputed regularly to inform the Secretariat of State of the congregation's actions, did so too on that very day. The results were not slow in coming. They turned the mood from quiet euphoria into surprise and deep dismay.

Missed Signals

The news of the indicative or straw vote upset the Pope greatly. The first reaction came the next day, January 23, in the form of a letter to Father General from the secretary of state, whom the Pope had expressly commissioned to write it. The General made the letter known to the congregation immediately. A plenary session was scheduled for the following day to address the whole matter, especially the questions raised by the letter itself.

The secretary of state, Cardinal Villot, emphasized that the mind of the Pope had been communicated to the General by his earlier letter of December 3 and by word of mouth, and that this ought to have been made known to the delegates. This reference to word-of-mouth intervention was news to the congregation. The cardinal on to say that since his December 3 letter was public and since the oral explanation later given removed any doubt about the correct interpretation of that letter and about the mind of the Pope, it should have been a major duty of the General to take steps to deflect the congregation from moving toward positions or decisions not in conformity with the Pope's attitude. This latter remark caused yet further surprise to the delegates, since it seemed to imply a fundamental misunderstanding of the position of the general in a general congregation. He presides, his opinions are taken very seriously, his influence is great; but he is not in any sense the master of the congregation and he cannot order it to take or omit any action. The cardinal declared that the Pope wished to receive a written report of the reasons that the delegates had adduced for choosing the direction indicated in the straw vote. He told the General that he should take care that the congregation refrain from any deliberations contrary to the norms of the cardinal's earlier letter of September 1973 and the papal address of December 3, 1974, at the beginning of the congregation, and that profession of four vows continue to be available only under the conditions then in force.

A long and complicated plenary session took place on January 24. The General set forth the background to Cardinal Villot's letter, assisted in so doing by two of the members of the congregation who had worked with him in the measures about to be described here. As the General told it, in the early evening of December 17, soon after the commissions had been set up, the General, together with those two delegates who were officially and intimately involved in the work of the congregation, went on an unofficial and confidential visit to the secretary of state. It was unofficial because they were in no sense representing the congregation; it was confidential because they wanted to leave to the Pope and the secretary of state full freedom to respond or not. They told the cardinal that it looked as if the congregation was inclined to deal fundamentally with grades. In view of that, they asked whether, despite the remarks of the Pope, the congregation could in a hypothetical case apprise the Pope of the reasons for which the congregation might make a request of the Holy See on the matter of changing the present legislation on grades, always presuming the two-thirds majority vote necessary in such a case.

They made clear to the secretary that the congregation was completely willing to accede to the wishes of the Pope. At the same time, they told him of the great number of postulata from province congregations on the question of grades. They gave reasons why it seemed to them not prudent to forbid any discussion of the matter right at the beginning of the congregation. Briefly put, those reasons were as follows: First, it would damage the morale of the congregation itself if it could not discuss what it thought good and, indeed, necessary to discuss. Second, it might not be good that the Pope enter into the matter even before he could know what the congregation really thought. Third, it would not be good for the Society as a whole if the moral authority of the congregation, the Society's highest governing body, were to be reduced or nullified right at the beginning of the meeting. With all this in mind, the secretary's visitors asked if the congregation could present to the Pope its reasons, should it decide to move ahead on the possibility of granting the profession of four vows to all Jesuits. The secretary of state replied that he did not wish to respond personally, that he thought the Pope's mind was already rather well made up; but he promised to let the Pope know of this visit and of the question. All agreed that there was to be no news of the visit.

Several days later, just before Christmas, the secretary of state asked the General to come to his office or to send someone in his place. The General sent one of the men who had accompanied him on the prior visit. On return he reported to the General the details of the meeting. The secretary had asked him at the meeting to read a note on his desk which stated that the Pope wanted matters to remain as they were and as expressed in the secretary's letter of December 3. Judging that the note which he had just read was not directly responsive to the request made at the visit several days earlier, the General's representative had then asked directly whether or not the congregation could discuss the question of grades with a view to changing present legislation. He informed the secretary that it was hard for anyone other than the congregation itself to exclude anything from its work. Cardinal Villot replied that he himself could not and did not wish to comment at all on the note. All parties had wished to keep the matter confidential, even though some rumors were beginning to seep around the corridors of the Vatican. Still, the delegate who was the General's representative promised to do everything to maintain confidentiality, and said that it was his impression that such was also the mind of the secretary. He reported fully to the General what had taken place.

At this point, after the preceding account of the facts as the General understood them, both of the delegates who had accompanied him corroborated the details just given by Fr. Arrupe. One of them remarked that certainly after the first meeting with the secretary of state he had had no doubt about the mind of the Pope on the question of grades, but that he had felt bound by the secrecy imposed upon all participants in the meeting. The General and the other delegate also agreed at that time that they were indeed bound by secrecy. This obviously presented problems. The main one was given as an example. When in the usual course of conversation about grades among the members of the congregation (who knew nothing of the visit), someone would happen to ask the General or either of his two companions what he thought personally was the mind of the Pope, each tried to indicate it as well as he could without saying anything that might reveal the meetings upon whose confidentiality they had all agreed.

There was the nub of the problem. "Confidentiality" for the Jesuits who were privy to the situation embraced both the fact and the substance of the conversations, including that from those conversations they personally had learned definitively the mind of the Pope. "Confidentiality" for the secretary of state included the fact of the conversations, but not the substance. Hence, when the straw votes were taken, the Holy See was outraged because it considered both that the Pope's mind was eminently clear and that the congregation had had every reason to know it. The three men who had visited the secretary of state were caught in the middle of several conflicting responsibilities as they understood them. They regarded as beyond question both the mind of the Pope and the obligation not to reveal how they had acquired such certainty. The General himself was stretched out between a rock and a hard place in seeming to disregard the wishes of the Holy See, both because he too thought himself bound by the confidential nature of the conversations and because the Holy See did not seem to understand the position of the General vis-à-vis the congregation itself.

The members of the congregation were now by turns and in varying degrees surprised, puzzled, amazed, angry, dismayed. They were surprised, obviously, because this was the first they knew of the visit with the secretary of state. They were puzzled at the mutual incomprehension of what each of the two parties had understood by the words of the other. They were amazed that the secretary of state and presumably the Pope as well seemingly misunderstood the General's position in the congregation and apparently were unaware of what "representation" meant in the Society. They were angry at the blame which the letter imputed to the General and at what seemed to many the inability or unwillingness of the Holy See to make clear and direct statements of intent or to answer clearly the question, May we present reasons for a change? Some thought that the members of the congregation were not being treated like responsible adults but like errant schoolboys. Finally, they were dismayed at the position in which the congregation now found itself in relation to the Pope.

The General then opened the session to any and all comments from the floor. They ranged across the whole situation. Some asked about the implications of "representation." Several requested to know what the Pope's reasons were for refusal to allow change or even discussion of change, and how he might have been influenced to that decision. The General did not know; the

Pope had told him nothing. Many wondered how to explain the situation to the Society (and to the press). Bluntly asked were questions about breaches of confidentiality in the congregation itself. Proposals were tentatively advanced on how to correct misinterpretations. Each of the questions the General answered; each of the comments he acknowledged by a response. To the remark on confidentiality he replied that it was the obligation of each delegate to ask how he himself was fulfilling that responsibility among adult mature Jesuits. Furthermore, he added that most fundamentally the delegates had to have confidence in each other, for without that the congregation simply would not function. Lastly, the General spoke movingly about considering the situation with serenity and seeing in it the Lord's gift of the cross. He tried to point out the unexpected ways in which God fulfilled desires, in that through this painful episode the congregation, now at the explicit wish of the Pope, had the very opportunity it had sought, to give to the Pope its reasons for action on the question of grades. The General's remarks and the spirit in which he made them were of great importance in calming the mood of the congregation.

A group of delegates was deputed to prepare for the Pope a full account of the actions of the congregation on the question of grades and the reasons for them. Several days later a draft of it occupied the delegates in another plenary session, after they had had the opportunity to consider it in assistancy meetings. When revised, it went to the Holy See. Basically but at greater length it set forth what has earlier been recounted in this study. It gave a historical background and a detailed account of the reasons, one by one, given against and for changes.

In reply, Pope Paul on February 15 sent a personally written letter to Father General stating that there could be no changes in the matter of the fourth vow and asking that all the decrees of the congregation be sent to him before they were published. There was no way, of course, that the press would not know these decisions of the Pope. The *Times* of London, *Le Monde* in Paris, the *Corriere della Sera* of Milan, and the *New York Times* were among the papers that made it headline news, often somewhat simplified in the text if not sensationalized in the headlines.[42]

Five days later, on the morning of February 20, Fr. Arrupe had a meeting with the Pope, about which he reported to the congregation that afternoon. It had not been an easy encounter. The Pope had been very perturbed at the actions of the congregation. He regarded himself as the "custodian" or guardian of the Society's Institute *(custos Instituti)*. The essential point made at the meeting was that there was to be no legislation extending the

---

[42] For example, the headlines in the *New York Times* read "Pope Paul Vetoes Jesuits' Reforms: Democratization Move in Order Meets Resistance from the Vatican" (*New York Times*, Feb. 28, 1975).

fourth vow. He regarded fidelity of Jesuits to himself as fidelity to themselves. He was surprised that the congregation had not understood him and had not seen his talk at the beginning of the meeting as a program for its action. He viewed the possible change in grades as damaging to the *Formula of the Institute,* particularly because, according to him, it would change the distinctive characteristic of the Society as a presbyteral order. He was also concerned that such a change might be connected with certain theological theories about the nature of the priesthood and with a thrust toward promoting justice that could undermine directly priestly ministries if it put undue emphasis on the political and social involvement of priests. This would be to the detriment of tasks proper to the layperson and the priest alike. He felt that the congregation had not paid enough attention up to the present to the spiritual and religious life. He added that there had been deviations in doctrine and discipline with regard to the hierarchy and the teaching authority of the Church during the period since the last congregation. The Pope stressed his willingness to see the General at any time. Later, the General emphasized again and again to the delegates that it was clear to him that the Pope genuinely loved the Society and hoped for great assistance from it in the difficult times that lay ahead.

For the members of the congregation, the previous several weeks, from the papal reaction at the straw vote on grades to this visit of the Pope and the General, had been a very difficult time. St. Ignatius in the *Spiritual Exercises* speaks of "consolation without cause." Those weeks from late January to that present time could have been described spiritually as a period of "desolation with cause." Popularly they could have been characterized by the term "depression." There was not the least doubt that the delegates had great respect for the Holy Father and quite deeply wanted to maintain that respect. They were happy to appeal to motives of faith in accepting his decision and they had no desire to disturb or embarrass him by their actions. Yet clearly he was disturbed. This was enough to disturb them in turn.

Equally conducive to this mood of dejection was the way in which, after a reasonable examination of the facts before them, they could not help but perceive the reaction of the Holy See. A serious group of men had been chosen by their brethren and, through postulata from all over the world, had been firmly enjoined by the Society itself to deal with a subject of great importance. They were now told that they should have known not to deal with it at all, that they were forbidden to treat the subject any further, that even the tentative treatment which in good faith they had so far accorded to the subject was a possible manifestation of even more widespread problems, and that the person who presided at their meeting and whom they greatly respected had neglected a clear duty to turn them away from a consideration of the subject of grades. It was especially difficult to understand that a decision on a matter so important to the Society had been arrived at even before the Society's representatives had gathered to discuss the matter. Who in the Society was more legitimately placed than they to give to the Pope reasons for actions that the Society had asked them to consider? Innocently unaware of the Pope's attitude, they had taken up the matter, only to let him know a tentative judgment of the congregation and to present it to him as a possibility. But now the prohibition to continue even this had implied that they were incapable of making an informed judgment about the Society and its needs. The delegates could not help wondering about the unofficial sources of information and advice to the Pope that might have led to his antecedently unknown judgment and to his present reaction.

As a result, there were ambivalent feelings of dismay at failing to know the wishes of the Pope, anger at the way in which those wishes had been transmitted, and bafflement at how he could have acquired impressions that would lead to his decision to cut off consideration before it even began. All of this to varying degrees had an obvious effect on members of the congregation. For some delegates it was a very deep experience of spiritual desolation. In other ways, too, the effects of the situation were evident. The work of the congregation was tiring enough in itself, but an even heavier physical weariness fell upon many of the members. They recognized the temptation to impatience brought on by the strain of this whole affair, and attempted to counter it by being at times almost elaborately polite to each other. Previously there had been minor illnesses among so large a group of men; the number and variety of such illnesses increased perceptibly in these weeks. Whatever had led the Pope to think that the delegates were prone to alter the Society fundamentally and whoever had helped to convey the mistaken impression had done a great disservice to the congregation, to the Society, and to the Pope himself. Fortunately for the congregation, it had in the General a person who calmed its spirit, encouraged its devotion, brought it out of its discouragements, and led it to carry on its responsibilities with as much serenity as was then possible.

Eventually the work of the commission on formed members or grades was embodied in the very brief eighth decree of the congregation and in several paragraphs of the official historical preface to the acts of the congregation. The decree laid "very great stress on promoting the unity of vocation of the entire body of the Society, as enshrined in our Constitutions," and asked "each and every member to make this unity shine forth" and "to ensure that grades be not a source of division."[43] It also commended and urged that the "participation of the temporal coadjutors in the life and apostolic activity of the Society be further promoted" and that "the norms for the promotion of priests to the profession of four vows, better adapted by the Thirty-first General Congregation to today's circumstances, be put into practice."[44]

---

[43] GC 32, D. 8:1 [191].
[44] Ibid., D. 8:2 [192].

The three paragraphs in the historical preface were themselves the subject of brief but spirited comments. A first draft had included the remark that the congregation had not wished to treat of the subject of grades. Several members of the congregation pointed out in the assembly with some vigor, not to say heat, that that statement simply was not in accord with the facts and as such could hardly be voted for with any personal integrity. So the three paragraphs confined themselves to stating that the congregation had subjected to careful examination those postulates dealing with the question of grades, that it had presented the whole question, together with their reasons, to the Holy See, that since the Pope had expressed his will that the fourth vow should remain reserved, the congregation "accepted the decision of His Holiness obediently and faithfully," and that the congregation wanted by means of the eighth decree to "continue to strengthen the unity of vocation of all our members."[45] Much remained unsaid.

Our Mission Today

Meanwhile, of course, other work had to go on even in the midst of the January and February reactions to the Holy See. So it did, but in a rather troubled atmosphere. Fortunately, on the next major topic much had been done in some serenity before the storms of late January. On the twenty-fourth of that month, the delegates had all received a draft text of almost fifty pages entitled "Our Mission Today." It was to be the object of vigorous debate, rigorous questions, detailed explanations, and ultimately of very helpful suggestions on how to handle the topic itself and the draft text. That text had emerged from the joint work, earlier mentioned, of the three Commissions on Apostolic Orientations and Criteria, on Our Mission and Apostolic Obedience, and on Promoting Justice in the World. For the rest of the congregation the document to be proposed was the product of those three groups.

At its very beginning the text took note of its literary form. It was not so much a juridical decree as it was a message of guidance and inspiration to Jesuits everywhere. What it was proposing could not come about as the result of legislation but of insight and conversion. It tried to avoid theological positions still in dispute and it wished to look at the implications of a fundamental option to serve the faith and to promote justice in a context that was simultaneously biblical, theological, and Ignatian. The five central chapters dealt with the contemporary world and the Jesuit mission, service of the faith, promotion

---

[45] GC 32, "Historical Preface," 15. As a matter of fact, the total membership the congregation, with the exception of fewer than a dozen, had in the straw vote responded affirmatively to the question of whether the congregation should deal with the subject of grades, and almost three-quarters of the delegates, again in the straw votes, had opted for the possibility of simply abolishing grades.

of justice as an apostolic priority, choices of apostolic activity in that perspective, and, finally, a "body for the mission," or the possibilities of a corporate oneness across the multiform apostolic endeavors of the Society.

After an oral introduction of the text to the whole assembly, assistancy groups met and focused on a set of fifteen propositions provided by the joint commission. Reactions from the assistancies were thoughtful but direct and even blunt. Among such reactions were the following: What the document wished to do was worthy of praise and basically so were its contents. But it was too long and diffuse; it did not adequately integrate the two components of the service of faith and the promotion of justice; it wandered back and forth between a gospel sense and a socio-economic sense of "justice"; it did not highlight adequately the spiritual component of this concern or task; it imperiled the priestly character of the Society; it embroiled the Society in partisan and ideological politics. As if that were not enough, particular words or phrases were judged to be ambiguous, wrongheaded, contrary to fact, or pejorative.

Then individual delegates had their say after those kind words from the twelve assistancy reporters. Prior to the actual debate, twenty-seven delegates had asked to speak; one mercifully abstained when he heard his views already propounded; twelve more delegates asked in the course of the debate to have their say. The multiplicity of comments revolved around three main concerns: the priestly character of Jesuit endeavors, the ambiguities of political involvement, and the frailty of the theological and spiritual underpinnings for the weighty structure and stressful activities that the document proposed.

The concerns about priestly character centered on the document's supposed confusion, sometimes explicit but more often implicit, between the specifically ministerial priesthood and the more general priesthood common to all the faithful, and on the unacknowledged shifts back and forth between the two. But that concern became entangled with another problem. Were activities on behalf of faith and justice necessarily first to be directed to the individual conversion of hearts or at least concomitantly to changes in social structure? Questions of priesthood need not logically be caught up with questions of individual and society, but in this debate they were. On this same question, some delegates pointedly noted that a change of heart from sin to virtue does not necessarily bring a change of structure from oppressive to beneficent. Saints have been known to support, with a completely innocent ignorance, social structures that were viciously oppressive.

The question of political involvement drew comments and questions just as blunt. Was political involvement priestly? Why was it less priestly than intellectual or academic involvement? Should not such involvement be left to laymen? ("Laywomen" was not used; sex-inclusive language was not yet a conscious concern of the delegates.) Why not distinguish civic-action groups from political parties? Some pointed out with the anguish of experience that opponents of any change in an oppressive social structure would not allow such a distinction; any amelioration of the lot of the oppressed is all too facilely regarded as political subversion. (No one could forget that the congregation included delegates from other than Western democracies.) No matter what the actual circumstances, could the Society really stay silent without abdicating all right to be taken seriously in a world of pressing moral and pastoral responsibilities?

A large number of the delegates were convinced that the theological and spiritual bases for whatever the Society did in the area of faith and justice had to be set down as a firm foundation for such activity.[46] Other delegates were uneasy with what seemed to them an avoidance of the awful and obvious facts of the unjust and degrading condition in which a great part of humankind could barely exist. They worried about the comfortable ease, attested by experience, with which theological statements and pious platitudes could tranquilize even the fervent Christian and the committed Jesuit.

The coordinator of the further work on this document had to be optimistic indeed who, at the end of the debate, said that there were some clear points of convergence; and anyone had to be fairly rash who said that he expected to return later for straw votes on several points which would bring consensus. In the event, the coordinator was proven right.

The Congregation Still in Session

Near the end of January 1975, after about two months in session, the congregation again looked carefully down the distance. It looked at the road that led to its goals and how it was to sprint or trudge toward them without being too often nudged off the path or delayed on the journey. The topic of governance had not yet come to the floor. Questions on final vows and tertianship were yet unresolved. The poverty document had yet to have a full debate. How best to respond to the papal concerns was in the background. And always intrusive, whether one wanted it to be or not, was the simple question: When is it all going to end?

If the pace of this present narrative both moves somewhat faster and yet seems to circle back to concerns already dealt with at length, it does so because such was now the rhythm of the congregation. Many of the major issues had had agonizingly detailed first presentations and had gone back out of sight for further development in the light of the responses they had received. Now those issues appeared on stage again, but they could be dealt with more quickly, with the final results embodied in the actual decrees of the congrega-

---

[46] It did become theologically a little complicated when one delegate got to "justice" only by starting with the internal processions of the Trinity.

tion. Some other issues of importance since the very beginning of the congregation had yet to be treated even for the first time in plenary session. A few issues
were even now new but pressing. Some questions simply would not be treated
at all, and that for several reasons. Either they were matters pertinent not to the
congregation but to the General, or they were not yet mature enough, or, in
simple fact, they were not important enough to keep more than two hundred
Jesuits from all over the world in session longer than necessary.

Additional Priorities

Late in January the General and his council had given the delegates a
list of forty-one topics drawn from the postulata. These topics had not earlier
been set for priority treatment in the congregation, but they had been subjects
of ongoing work on the part of various commissions. Now the delegates were
asked to indicate which of those topics should yet be dealt with as priority
items. Four of the topics gained more than two-thirds of the positive votes of
those responding. Those topics were then put on the priority agenda. Three of
them involved governance. The governance questions included the matter of
general assistants, regional assistants, and a council for the general; it included as
well the size and the frequency of general congregations, the participation of the
nonprofessed in future congregations, and the revision of the formulas or rules
of procedure for the various types of congregations. The fourth item dealt with
final vows and tertianship. Besides these new priority items, the other central
topics, of course, would be coming back to the floor in the form of definitive
proposals ready for a final debate and, as the delegates fervently hoped, a final
vote.

On January 28 and 29, the material on the structure of the central
government of the Society came up for discussion. Among the questions dealt
with in its report were the following: How was the General's "council" best to
be used? How better ensure communication and cooperation among the general
consultors, the regional assistants (now twelve), and the expert consultants in
particular areas. The right hand of the curia, as was true of any organization
that large, had its own problems knowing what the left hand was doing.
Further questions dealt with the number of officials and the length of their
terms of office, and with the possibility of commissioning a study of the
structure and functioning of the curia, possibly to be carried out even by
outside experts.[47] All the assistancies discussed the material in small-group

---

[47] This last suggestion was more unusual than might at first appear. For example, in
all the preparations for the Thirty-first and Thirty-second General Congregations, it would
seem, no formal or explicit suggestion was ever made to use outside consultants. In the actual
administration of the two congregations, the Society seems never to have considered even the
possibility that persons or agencies which were not Jesuit might be of assistance.

sessions. Then the whole long morning and afternoon sessions of January 31 were very unusual exercises. Delegates from all over the world were invited to question the General at length, and his general consultors and principal officials as well, on the central government of the Society, and to make comments on how best to improve its administrative functioning. After the General had presented his comments, he left the congregation hall so that the delegates could treat with full frankness questions and matters which might touch him personally.

"Communication" was the opening byword. There seemed to be real need for greater communication among all groups and across all lines in the curia. Next came the rather obvious need not to let the urgency of the immediate get in the way of the importance of long-range planning for the Society. The number of assistancies and regional assistants came in for question. One delegate from the Far East remarked, to the evident surprise of some of his Western brethren, that if one assistancy sufficed for all the nations of Southeast Asia, he could not see why so many assistancies were needed for Europe! The suggestion of a management study of the curia by outside experts was seconded. Emphasis was placed on the necessity of assigning men to the curia who were capable of working as a team.

A series of easy votes gave to the commission clear indications of the mind of the congregation. The previous congregation's legislation on assistants and consultors needed improvement. Legislation was to provide for a specific council for regular consultation. The general assistants were to act as general and canonical consultors. There were to be at least six general consultors, and the General could name as such men who were not general assistants. General consultors were to have responsibility for certain sectors of the Society's life or work. A limit, usually of no more than eight years, was to be placed on a consultor's term of office. An outside study and review of the current international secretariats was simply suggested to the General. One proposal which was not accepted was that there should be a general consultor who would serve as coordinator of the activities of the curia, somewhat on the model of an executive or administrative vice-president. The final document that eventually resulted, decree 15 of the congregation, on the central government of the Society, included substantially all of the points agreed to in these straw votes.

Poverty Again

As February, the third month of the meeting, came around, the congregation once again turned its attention to poverty. Round and round it went in a circle that soon became as twisted as a pretzel when a juridical controversy, further complicated by a procedural controversy, threatened to entangle the whole subject. To begin with the simple facts, the draft decree had two parts, the pastoral and the juridical. Edward Sheridan, the English assistant and chairman of the commission, who had worked for years on the subject, introduced the pastoral part. Urbano Navarrete, professor of canon law at the Gregorian University, introduced the juridical. Together they and their subcommissions had had to consider three hundred pages of comments from the delegates. As if that were not enough, more was yet to come. After quite careful and clear introductions, the congregation voted to hold a discussion on February 3. Over the intervening weekend a scruple which some few experienced came to the forefront.

Before the story of the appearance and resolution of that scruple, the pastoral aspects of the document should be noted, since the juridical elements have earlier been dealt with in this history on pages 40 and 41. The introduction recalled the meaning of poverty in the context of the Gospels and of the Spiritual Exercises, noted the present circumstances in the world, the Church, and the Society that called for Jesuit commitment to religious poverty, and reminded the congregation of the connection between this subject and the commitment to the promotion of justice. These circumstances were meant to have consequences in the Society's legislation affecting current realities and the Society's practice in regard to a simple lifestyle. That practice was to touch both individuals and communities. For individual Jesuits it would imply an honest day's work, authenticity, love of the poor, and work with and for them. For Jesuit communities it would mean resources devoted not to their own good but to that of the apostolate. For all, individuals as well as communities, it would imply fraternity across personal and provincial and national lines. For successful practice it would require both conversion of heart and revision of law.

The entangling scruple was brought to the attention of the congregation before extended discussion began. Briefly put, the proposed legislation set up a new distinction between a Jesuit apostolic work or institutionalized apostolate and a Jesuit community, and indicated some consequences expected to result from it. Were this distinction and those consequences in conflict with the *Formula of the Institute* of the Society and with the Constitutions? Obviously the commission proposing this legislation did not think so. It had already reviewed the whole question. So had the special juridical commission of the present congregation. It had decided by a vote of four to one that there was no problem and that there was no doubt. But some still doubted. Several distinguished canonists doing preparatory work on the material had seen no difficulties at all. Several distinguished experts disagreed; they thought that the proposed legislation certainly went against the Constitutions and probably against the *Formula.*

If this view was correct, that the proposal "touched the Institute," the congregation first had to have a majority vote even to discuss the issue; then it had to have a two-thirds affirmative vote to decree anything new; then it had to go to the Holy See for approval of such a change. However—and this was a very important "however"—if there was a theoretical doubt about the meaning of the *Formula* or the Constitutions in a particular matter, then a general congregation had the unquestionable right to declare authoritatively what the *Formula* or the Constitutions meant. So, this congregation could, if it so wished, by a simple majority and without further recourse to the Holy See, decide what the fundamental legislation of the Society meant in this matter. What did the congregation want to do? As a preliminary step, it wanted to hear the pros and the cons simply put.

On the afternoon of February 3, two canonists, Pedro Abellán, procurator general of the Society, and the previously mentioned Urbano Navarrete, presented and debated the issue before the whole congregation. For some of the delegates it summoned up shades of long-gone oral disputations! Abellán insisted that there were grounds for a true doubt and that the congregation would most prudently go to the Holy See. Navarrete argued the opposite side of the question: There was no infringement of the Institute and no doubt about it at all. Then came the voting. In two ballots the congregation decided by a very substantial majority that the distinction of Jesuit apostolic work and Jesuit community was not certainly against the *Formula* or Constitutions. Then, substantial majorities declared that there was a doubt about the meaning of the *Formula*. Then a majority voted to take the route of making an authoritative declaration of the meaning of the *Formula* and the Constitutions in order to remove the doubt about their meaning. And there was no doubt at all that the congregation could do this. A vote on the text of such an authoritative declaration would be taken the next day, February 4. But then, before the session came to an end, some delegates challenged the vote just taken on procedural and substantive grounds.

There was a way to resolve the challenge. The congregation had a commission on procedure. On the evening of that same February 3, that commission took great care in going over all the activities of the day. The next morning the secretary of the congregation told the delegates that the committee on procedure, after that careful review, had found both the procedure and the vote valid. But because some delegates had said that even after the explanations given before the vote, they had still been confused when voting, the commission recommended that the General allow the vote to be repeated. After taking advice from the council of the congregation, he agreed. Then, before the repetition of the vote, the General told the congregation that after thinking and praying about it, he personally thought that the wiser move might be to go the way of a two-third vote and subsequent recourse to the Holy See—even though he was convinced that the proposed legislation was good and what the Society needed—and that he hoped that when it came up for a final vote on the last draft, it would be approved overwhelmingly, so that it would also gain approval of the Holy See.

Perhaps because of these comments, perhaps because the delegates were at this point understandably gun-shy of possible Vatican reactions, the congregation now voted on the morning of February 5 to reverse its previous decision to use its right to make an authoritative declaration of the meaning of the *Formula* and of the Constitutions in this matter. So no declaration was made.

Just two weeks later, on February 18 and 19, the final text of the document on poverty came to a definitive and overwhelming vote of approval in the congregation. It consisted of the two previously mentioned pastoral and juridical sections. The purpose of the document in making quite definite changes in the Society's administration of its material goods was, as the document explicitly states, to strengthen and confirm the individual and communal practice of poverty in the Society. This was to be done not simply by pious exhortations but by a combination of long-needed structural changes and a clear statement that it is the law of the Spirit which would best interpret statutes.

The delegates enjoyed—if that is the word—a vivid example of how much effort a process could take as they conducted the final balloting on the document on poverty. That process alone occupied more than four hours as the congregation cast a total of 153 ballots on specific amendments, on each section of each of the two parts of the document, on each of the two parts as such, and finally on the decree as a whole. Although there were other periods to rival it, this was probably the longest single block of time devoted exclusively to the activity of voting. That may have been appropriate: besides the topic of poverty, no other issue had claimed more time, calculated in months and years, devoted to research, consultation, discussion, and debate throughout the Society before the congregations could reach their decisions.

The congregation in sending its documents to the Holy See did have formal "recourse" for approval of this legislation. The Pope in the letter of May 2, 1975, from the Cardinal Secretary of State did approve the legislation on poverty and asked the next congregation to reexamine it "against the background of experience gained in the years ahead."[48] All this constitutes the background to the questions about the legislation on poverty that were addressed in 1983 to each of the province congregations in preparation for the Thirty-third General Congregation and for the definitive confirmation of that legislation by the congregation.[49]

This whole matter was a good example, one among many, of how the members of the congregation regularly went to extraordinary lengths to ensure that the voices of a minority were taken into account in discussion, deliberation, and procedure. It was also a good example of the problems raised when a

---

[48] GC 32, Document V, Letter of the Cardinal Secretary of State to Father General, May 2, 1975, p. 546.

[49] GC 32, D. 2 [56–59].

large group of men assemble only at lengthy intervals, particularly when the participants are inexperienced even in the rather normal procedures used by deliberative bodies to assure a smooth and orderly flow of business. And while scruples need to be taken seriously in themselves, and surely were in this instance, they were also an indication of how lack of awareness of the history of the Society could foster a caution that makes for immobility.

Tertianship and Final Vows

Not at all an example of immobility was the progress that now took place on the work of the tenth commission, dealing with tertianship and final vows. Even though it had not been in the list of items for priority treatment, the congregation approved its coming to the floor. One reason among others may have been the realization among the delegates that there were throughout the Society at the time more than eight hundred priests who had been ordained more than three years and had not yet made tertianship.

The draft text recommended not requiring one to be thirty-three years old in order to take final vows, that the ten years of membership required for priests before final vows could include the years spent in philosophy and theology, and that priests and brothers make tertianship together. It proposed two models for tertianship. In the first or *A* model, tertianship would be made in the year after theology was completed, with the long retreat in its early months, followed by ordination to the diaconate and priesthood, to be followed by supervised apostolic work, with final vows coming at the end of that year. The *B* model followed more closely the current practice of theology, ordination, apostolic work for several years, tertianship, and final vows. A third proposal would allow both *A* and *B* models in the same province or region. The assistancy groups were in close agreement on the proposals for final vows but they disagreed on the desirability and applicability of the models. The chairman promised that the commission would swiftly review all proposed amendments, and hoped that a definitive text could quickly be submitted to a vote.

The commission fulfilled his promise. Within a very few days, on February 8, a final draft of the document came to the floor. After being more than two months in session, the congregation experienced for the very first time the sense of accomplishment in bringing the whole process of producing a decree to a specific conclusion. It took fifteen votes on formal amendments and ten definitive votes on specific parts of the document to do so. As that last approving vote registered on the tally board and as the General raised and held aloft the hand of the chairman of the commission's editorial committee, everyone broke into applause; and the comments in every language could be reduced essentially to a single one: See, it can be done! The material as finally approved is contained in the congregation's two brief decrees on tertianship and on final vows.[50]

Permanent Deacons

One other question of juridical status had to be dealt with. The Thirty-first Congregation had made possible the existence of permanent deacons in the Society, following upon Vatican II's restoration of this order. At that time the Holy See had yet to make clear how this order was to apply to religious. It had done so in the intervening years and had then asked religious orders and congregations to determine the juridical status of their permanent deacons. This congregation did so in decree 9, specifying that those Jesuits who are ordained permanent deacons "will retain the grade that they already have in the Society." Approved temporal coadjutors could become formed temporal coadjutors; scholastics could, by way of exception, be admitted by the General to the grade of spiritual coadjutor.[51]

How to Proceed?

A few days before the definitive vote on tertianship and final vows, a request had come to the General to put in motion the machinery for setting a target date for the conclusion of the congregation. A discussion on February 5 showed more than enough frustration at the pace of the congregation. But it also showed some who believed that all the time available was needed for thoughtful care in the work yet to be done. More voting, as usual, took place. A large majority wanted measures taken to limit debate and to facilitate less important matters. That the delegates meant business was clear when on February 6 they did something that a congregation is often reluctant to do. They gave to definitors the task of preparing the text for changes in the formula or procedural handbook for province congregations. "Definitors" are a small group or task force of members of a general congregation chosen by the delegates and given power either definitively to settle (along with the General) a particular item of business or to draft a text to be brought back to the congregation for a final vote. Such a text, however, is not subject to amendment by the congregation and has simply to be accepted or rejected. The willingness to make use of definitors was an indication of the growing feeling that a halt had to be called sometime and that that time could not be too far in the future. Fortunately for morale, no one ventured to predict what really happened, that the congregation would be in session for yet another month. And just a few days after agreeing to appoint definitors on one subject, the congregation turned

---

[50] GC 32, Decs. 7 and 10 [187–90 and 196–98].
[51] GC32, D. 9 [193–95].

down the proposal to appoint them for another, the subject of Jesuit spiritual and community life.

Jesuit Community Life and Jesuit Identity

The commission on spiritual and community life, which was responsible for treating of Jesuit religious life, had to concern itself with postulata of the most diverse kind. They dealt with the spiritual life in general and in particular, with discernment, obedience, pluralism, unity, members, community, rules, prayer, superiors, and almost any subject that touched on the internal life of the Society. In what turned out to be a very successful attempt to develop a structure within which to treat such a variety of topics, the commission took its cue from the title of the eighth part of the Constitutions, "Helps toward Uniting the Distant Members with Their Head and among Themselves." From that beginning, it eventually developed decree 11, "Union of Minds and Hearts." It explicitly meant to approach Jesuit religious life as a phenomenon simultaneously personal and communitarian. The document was written to provide both an inspirational context and practical directives. Finally, it harked back again to that eighth part of the Constitutions in choosing as titles of its first three sections "Union with God in Christ," "Brotherly Communion," and "Obedience: the Bond of Union." A fourth and fifth section gave "Guidelines" and abrogated the "Common Rules," while commending to the General the publication of a summary of the decrees of the Thirty-first and Thirty-second General Congregations together with a summary of his letters to the Society. This summary could "serve as an index of principal features of our religious life."[52] Finally, a sixth section tried to make somewhat clearer that part of the Thirty-first Congregation's decree on obedience which dealt with possible conflicts between the dictates of conscience and the superior's will.[53]

In retrospect and when looked at as a whole, the final document is more orderly than the task of producing it turned out to be. Suggestions had come from every quarter when the commission had handed over to the congregation its first report, and now, in early February, its second report brought yet more comments. In addition to all this, the whole faith-justice orientation to the apostolic works of the Society would inevitably influence its religious life and the import of this document. Finally, the contretemps on grades roiled the waters and clouded the atmosphere. It was no wonder that discussion was long and earnest, contributed to even by those members who wanted the congregation to go about its business more quickly and expeditiously.

---

[52] GC 32, D. 11:54 [255].

[53] GC 32, D. 11:55 [256]. See also GC 31, D. 17:10 [279], for the original text to be clarified.

As usual, discussion on the report took place first in assistancy groups and then in plenary session. If all the individual comments on matters of minor importance were written down one by one, they would be more than this study could contain. Remarks of major importance, either because they came from assistancy groups or from several speakers or because of the subject matter, dealt with the supposedly excessive length of the text, the question of "daily" celebration of or participation in the Eucharist, the once again resurrected proposal for a required "hour of prayer," and the question of what to do about conscience difficulties in following an order. Lastly, the suggestion that the complications of subject and document might recommend having it revised by definitors received support from only one assistancy, no particular support from four of them, and strong reservations from seven. So, on February 7, after yet further debate, this time on how best to pose the question of what to do, the congregation gave its report back to the editorial committee of the eighth commission, mandating a drastic rewriting in the light of the comments it had heard over the previous days. The congregation did make one concession that indicated its fundamental trust of the editors, no matter how many comments those editors had had to listen to. The congregation decided that the complete revision would go to the delegates for formal written amendments and then, without further extended debate, be proposed for a final and definitive vote. That is exactly what happened later in the month.

Perhaps one of the most important statements in the document on union of minds and hearts as it came to be adopted by the congregation was its very first sentence. "The 32nd General Congregation confirms and commends the declaration and directives of the 31st General Congregation on the religious life contained in its Decrees 13–17 and 19."[54] It then gave the reason for such confirmation and commendation: "We believe them to be as helpful today in promoting our continual progress in spirit as when they were formulated, and hence they are implicitly assumed throughout the following statement."[55] It was no secret that in the Society there were some Jesuits, and outside the Society there were people of both high and ordinary station, who deemed the decisions of the previous congregation a mistake or even a disaster for Jesuit religious life. After the experience of almost nine years, even while clearly recognizing the problems that had arisen, the chosen representatives of the Society from around the world decisively affirmed otherwise.

---

[54] GC 32, D. 11:1 [199].
[55] Ibid.

General Assistants

As will be obvious throughout the rest of this account, the tempo of activity was accelerating. On Monday, February 10, the congregation voted approval to the changes proposed in late January regarding the structure of general assistants and consultors. Once that was done, within a few days, on February 14 and 15 at the end of the same week, the congregation elected four new general assistants.

The subcommittee on ordinary governance brought its revised text on general assistants and consultors to the plenary assembly together with eighteen formal amendments. The congregation voted to accept four of them. Then in the usual detailed but necessary procedure, it took fifteen separate votes to complete its work on that revised and amended text.[56] The decree essentially improved and confirmed the previous congregation's legislation on assistants and consultors of the general.[57] It also added to it provisions that, it hoped, would make consultation and communication easier for the Jesuits charged with the central administration and governance of the Society. A new provision made mandatory and automatic the election of general assistants whenever a general congregation was called, whether for the election of a general or for the transaction of major business. This last provision was not retroactive, but several weeks earlier the four general assistants then in office, Paolo Dezza, Vincent O'Keefe, Horacio de la Costa, and Jean-Yves Calvez, had signed and given to the congregation a joint postulatum asking that such an election be held now. The congregation in turn, now that it had passed the decree, took another vote on whether to proceed to such a new election of general assistants. The vote was affirmative. Two of the general assistants, Paolo Dezza and Horacio de la Costa, formally asked not to be considered for another term of office. The General decided to have the elections as soon as possible, after the four days of "murmuratio" or gathering information by and among the delegates about Jesuits who might be the best ones for such a post.

The elections took place on February 14 and 15. Two assistants were chosen on that first morning, one that afternoon, and the fourth on the next morning. Two were veterans in the job; two were new. Vincent O'Keefe was elected on the second ballot. He had been a delegate from the New York Province at the Thirty-first General Congregation and at that time had been elected a general assistant. He was the only one of the four chosen at that congregation who was to continue in office. Jean-Yves Calvez, elected on the

---

[56] As the voting sessions increased during this last month, the members could only bless the Lord in his creature electricity; for without the electronics of the tally board, the balloting procedures would have kept the meeting in session long beyond its eventual completion in March.

[57] GC 31, D. 44 [648–63].

fourth ballot, was from the Atlantic-France Province. He had been a general assistant since 1971. Immediately prior to that, he had been the first provincial of all France, a post established in 1968. He arrived at that position after being director of the Jesuit social-research center in Paris, Action Populaire; he came equipped with much experience in writing and lecturing on philosophy and political science, on the social teaching of the Church, and on Karl Marx. Cecil McGarry, elected on the third ballot, was present at the congregation as provincial of Ireland. He had studied moral theology at the Gregorian and taught the subject at the Jesuit theologate at Milltown Park in Ireland, where he had been rector and had involved himself in ecumenical endeavors. Parmananda Divarkar, elected on the fourth ballot, had come to the congregation by virtue of his office as the delegate of the General for all the Jesuit works common to the Indian Assistancy. He was a member of the Bombay Province, had studied in both India and Spain, had done doctoral work in philosophy, and had taught and been an administrator at St. Xavier's College and at the University of Bombay. He also had been involved in ecumenics and liturgy on a national scale in India.

Inculturation

The mention of a non-Western country such as India can serve to point up a problem and an opportunity for Jesuit life that this congregation was the first to address seriously, despite the fact that Jesuits had come from and lived in and worked with lands in all quarters of the globe. It was the opportunity and problem of what was first called "indigenization" and then later in the congregation "inculturation." In mid-January a group had been set up to reflect on and propose ways of dealing with the phenomena of adaptation as they related to community life and Jesuit formation, to philosophy and theology, and to intellectual and spiritual matters in contexts different from those of the developed lands of Europe and North America. Members of the commission came from the Assistancies of Africa, East Asia, Latin America, and India and from the Near East.

Its first report put in organized form the postulata that asked the congregation to take account of such inculturation. The topic had been an important one in the past year, 1974, at the synod of bishops treating evangelization, and the Society wanted to look at what it might do for and with the Church in areas of the world where the Church was young, or in a small minority, or undergoing rapid changes in self-understanding. The report was enlightening and helpful, but at this point few expected a specific document on the subject. It turned out otherwise. After two reports, and the presentation of a very brief text, the congregation adopted almost unanimously what is now the document on the work of inculturation of the faith and the promotion of Christian life. Its brevity is exceeded only by its importance for the possibilities it opens up both for the mission of the Society today and for the formation of Jesuits living in the midst of so many cultures other than those in which the Church and the Gospel have traditionally been incarnated.[58]

Formation

Formation of Jesuits has been an explicit concern of almost every general congregation in the history of the Society. This one was no different. The seventh commission introduced its text to the assembly on February 13. In two parts, one a reflection on formation and the other a series of directives or norms, the text dealt with three central concerns: formation for current apostolic needs, studies, and integration as the axis around which formation revolved, both initial and continuing.

Since every Jesuit has gone through formation in the Society, all Jesuits are at least tempted to think themselves experts in it. Some without good reason succumb to that temptation. Some are more modest in judging their own expertise. Remarks came from delegates of all three types—and understandably so, because the very future of the Society of Jesus is bound up so intimately with the present preparation of members who are linked to its authentic heritage and spirit and who will carry on its life and work imaginatively in the future. Most of the comments agreed with the document, but stressed one particular point or other that the speakers thought especially important. Among such points were the need to insist on excellence and the importance of serious learning, the need for adaptation in training in the very diverse cultures in which the Society exists, the importance of spiritual formation pari passu with academic and social formation, the encouragement of continuing education for older, experienced Jesuits, and, again, apostolic purpose and integration as the central themes of all formation. After all those words, the congregation had to decide on deeds. What was to follow and how was it to be done, given the fact that time was pressing? Despite the pressure, the congregation decided not to leave the subject untreated by a formal decree; and, just as in the case of religious and community life, it decided as well not to turn the task over to definitors. So back to the editorial committee went the task of drafting yet another text. That text came to be the basis for what we now have as the document entitled "The Formation of Jesuits, Especially with Regard to the Apostolate and Studies."[59]

The pressure of time put pressure on presence too. With the meeting so long in session, some delegates had to leave before its conclusion. They could do so only with permission of the congregation itself. Already at the end of

---

[58] GC 32, D. 5 [131–32].

[59] GC 32, D. 6 [133–90].

January five delegates had to receive that permission because of urgent responsibilities at home. As mid-February approached, two more left. Between then and the beginning of March, seventeen more members bade their adieux. And even in the last five days before the meeting finally ended on March 7, another seven delegates left the congregation. All in all, a total of thirty-one members departed during the course of the last six weeks. When the congregation began, it counted 236 members; on its last day there were 205. This could not fail to affect the work of the congregation. It surely made quite vivid the problems that were addressed by the commission on governance when it took up the question of the length, size, and periodicity of general congregations. That subject came to the floor in a second report on February 10; but because the subject went on being discussed until the very last day of the whole congregation, the treatment of it will come later in this account.

The Fourth Vow Again

One component of the specifically Jesuit identity is the fourth vow taken by the professed members of the Society. Granting it to a greater number of Jesuits or even further discussing such an extension had been forbidden by the Pope. But in its early sessions, the congregation commended to the deliberations of the fifth commission the history, the object, the meaning, and the import of the vow. Those subjects were still open to and, indeed, needed treatment, to judge from the postulata from the provinces. At the same time, the same commission was given the responsibility of dealing with the postulata on fidelity to the magisterium,[60] the way in which Jesuits ought to act in doctrinal matters, and the question of censures. Each of these questions, obviously, could influence all the others. Because the fourth vow itself had been agreed upon for priority treatment, the commission wanted to deal with it first and as a separate item.

On February 7 a rather succinct text came up for discussion. It stated clearly, right at the beginning, that when it spoke of the "meaning" of the fourth vow, it did not intend an authoritative declaration in the technical sense that the congregation had earlier discussed with reference to the document on poverty and its meaning in relation to the Constitutions or the *Formula of the Institute*. The report made clear that the vow had to be put in historical context. It suggested that Ignatius and the first companions had asked the Pope for

---

[60] The term "magisterium" seemed to have a variety of meanings in the postulata, and that added to the difficulties of a clear and adequate definition of what was being dealt with. Two very important French articles by Yves Congar, O.P., one a semantic history of the term "magisterium" and the other a brief history of the forms of "magisterium" and its relationship with teachers, are in an English translation in *The Magisterium and Morality*, ed. Charles E. Curran and Richard A. McCormick (New York: 1982).

guidance in order to make the choice of the most apt apostolate.[61] They then, according to the report, institutionalized this practice by adding the fourth vow to the traditional three vows of the religious life.

The object of the vow is "missions," or in present-day terms, "ministries" or "apostolates"; that is, the vow was "to go . . . wherever the popes may send us," and "to carry out whatever they may order which pertains to the progress of souls."[62] To the question as to whether that vow extended to doctrinal matters, some commentators expressed an opinion, not held by all, that clearly the vow itself did not deal with such matters. But it was at least possible to think of a pope giving to Jesuits with that vow a particular "mission" to teach or defend a doctrine, even a doctrine that is still legitimately controverted among competent theologians.[63] In any case, the spirit of the vow would urge a sincere attempt to interpret papal teaching as favorably as possible and to show respect for it. The reasons for the vow were still operative today, and the service of the universal Church would be made more efficacious through this special bond of union with the Pope.

---

[61] This reading of the sequence of intent and action is not universally accepted. For a differing view, see John W. O'Malley, S.J.'s recent essay, "The Fourth Vow in Its Ignatian Context," *Studies in the Spirituality of Jesuits* 15, no. 1 (January 1983): 45. He maintains that "any discussion of that vow that begins with Ignatius's esteem for the papacy instead of with the apostolic aims of the first companions has got things backward at the outset. . . . What came first was experience of ministry and a desire to exercise it in the most fruitful way possible. The companions only then decided on a vow *to that effect*, that is, on a vow 'to go wherever sent to do Christian ministry.'" However, both he and the author of the report in the congregation would agree completely on the prime necessity of serious historical studies in order to understand what Ignatius and the early Society meant by the fourth vow—especially if it is to make sense as "nuestro principio y principal fundamento" (*Cons.*, as cited in Monumenta Historica Societatis Iesu (MHSI) I:162; Ignatius wrote these words in 1545 in a sketch preliminary to the writing of the *Constitutions*, but they did not make their way into the *Constitutions* themselves) and to function for Jesuits today as a symbol of the "apostolic dynamism of the Society" (see O'Malley, "The Fourth Vow," 45). See also O'Malley's *The First Jesuits* (Cambridge: Harvard University Press, 1993), especially "The Papacy and the Popes," pp. 296–310.

[62] *The Formula of the Institute* of 1540 and again of 1550, *Cons.*, as cited in MHSI I:27f. and 377f., and also cited in English by O'Malley, "The Fourth Vow," 46f.

[63] Here too there is sharp current disagreement on whether the vow can extend to such a teaching or defense of a doctrine. See, for example, José García de Madariaga, S.J., "The Jesuits' Fourth Vow: Can It Extend to What He Teaches?" *Review for Religious* 41 (1982): 214–38, for an affirmative reply; for an opposing view, see John W. O'Malley, S.J., "The Fourth Vow." O'Malley's article, in footnote 7 on p. 50, gives references to the Spanish original of Madariaga's article and to other studies of this question in several languages. See also Antonio M. de Aldama, S.J., *The Formula of the Institute: Notes for a Commentary* (St. Louis: Institute of Jesuit Sources, 1990) and, by the same author, the *Constitutions of the Society of Jesus: An Introductory Commentary on the Constitutions* (St. Louis: Institute of Jesuit Sources, 1989).

The next day, February 8, the assistancy groups reported on their discussion of the document. Only a few seemed willing to accept the text as it stood. The way in which the document dealt with the question of the vow and its relation to doctrinal matters was the main point of concern. "Ambiguity," "confusion," "untenability" were among the terms used in the opinions expressed in the assistancy reports. Later on the same day and again in a further discussion on February 10, individual delegates expressed these same concerns. In addition, some expressed uncertainty whether any separate document on the fourth vow was at all opportune at the moment. Given the circumstances of the previous two months, perhaps such a document could only cause further problems of misinterpretation and misunderstanding. Eventually, on February 10, the congregation decided by quite a heavy majority vote that the text should be revised, resubmitted in that form for amendments from the delegates, and then brought to a vote.

A Letter from the Pope

A few days later, on February 15, Pope Paul VI wrote an autograph letter to Fr. Arrupe. In it he acknowledged receipt of "the account . . . of the reasons which moved the General Congregation in voting on the problem of grades and the fourth vow."[64] He confirmed his prohibition of any change related to it, worried about what he saw as "certain orientations and dispositions which are emerging from the work of the General Congregation," asked that the Society maintain and witness to its "spirituality and doctrine and discipline and obedience and service and example," exhorted the congregation "to consider seriously before the Lord the decisions to be made," and repeated "with fatherly alarm and utter seriousness: Think well, my dear sons, on what you are doing."[65] An earlier letter of September 1973 from the Pope and his address of December 3, 1974, at the opening of the congregation had dealt with faithfulness in doctrine and discipline toward the magisterium and the ecclesiastical hierarchy. The present letter in conjunction with that material rendered the whole subject far more delicate, wide-ranging, and complex than the congregation could ever adequately hope to deal with in the circumstances of uncertainty and weariness and misunderstanding in which it found itself.

With all this in mind and with the added pressure of time quite obvious, the General, in his responsibility as president of the congregation, took counsel with the general assistants recently elected and with the council of the president of the congregation on the schedule of affairs that that body still had to deal with. Given all those circumstances, he decided not to include a separate

---

[64] GC 32, Document III, Letter of Pope Paul VI to Father General, Feb. 15, 1975, pp. 539–41.

[65] Ibid., p. 540.

document on the fourth vow. On the other hand, he did take immediate steps to deal with the question of fidelity to the magisterium and to the Pope. The General asked five of the delegates each to write, in the context of the work already done by the fifth commission, a brief paper on thinking with the Church. Those five papers served as the basis for a single text that was then sent to the congregation for discussion in assistancy meetings and in full sessions. This subject as such had not yet been formally introduced into the agenda by the congregation's own agreed-upon procedures, so a vote was taken to do so. Then the members debated, decided on a very brief, particular decree on fidelity to the magisterium and the Supreme Pontiff, and gave time and space for amendments. A revised text came to the floor, and on the very last day of the whole meeting, March 7, voting took place on that text, which with several formal amendments is now decree 3 of the congregation. The fourth vow does not figure in the document. Rather, in the form of a declaration, the congregation acknowledges an obligation of reverence and fidelity to the magisterium and to the Supreme Pontiff and of proper responsibility to the Church, supports Jesuits engaged in the works of scholarship in the service of the Church, regrets failings, recommends the application of the norms of the Church and of the Society, and commends both the intelligent encouragement of freedom and the prevention and correction of failings in service to the faith and the Church.[66]

Jesuits Today

The declaration "Jesuits Today," which describes itself as "a response of the 32nd General Congregation to requests for a description of Jesuit identity in our time,"[67] is one of the last results of the work of the congregation.

After the working commissions had been set up at the beginning of the congregation, a kind of intercommission on "identity and charism" was established and charged with the task of keeping in touch with the work of the individual commissions and gathering from them the points that might emerge as central in describing the Jesuit charism as understood today. This group was to reflect on that material and to attempt to fashion it into a document, to be shared with all fellow Jesuits, that would depict those essential notes, that charism. On February 12 the intercommission made its first report and suggested seven possible forms under which a document on Jesuit identity might be developed. The examples presented ranged from an offering or oblation, to a profession of faith in the Society, to a prayer, to a contemporary reading of the *Formula of the Institute*, to a declaration. After some discussion, the delegates agreed that there should be such a document and that it should be in the form of a "declaration." For at least two reasons, no one was going to touch the

---

[66] GC 32, D. 3 [43–46].
[67] GC 32, D. 2:2 [11–42].

suggestion of a contemporary reading of the *Formula of the Institute*. First there was the Jesuit concern over the relations with the Holy See and the Pope's seeming conviction that the congregation was being tempted to tamper with the Institute. Secondly, such an attempt at a contemporary reading would have to summon up far more historical and textual expertise than the congregation at this point had the resources to command.

There was no lack of comments from delegates on what it meant to be a Jesuit today. The editorial group received almost one hundred suggestions for its text. The next draft, when proposed, received warmer acceptance than had probably any other document in the course of the congregation. "Friendly amendments" came its way as well as a few formal amendments. The general sentiment was to adopt the text almost as written, so that its combination of clear tone, refreshing vigor, roots in traditional Jesuit imagery, modern accent, and literary style as well as its content might come through unscathed. On March 1 the declaration received an almost unanimous vote, after the suggestion that the traditional "Suscipe" prayer be made its conclusion.

After that overwhelmingly favorable vote, two changes did take place. A delegate invoked the rather rare formal procedure of an "intercession," allowing further consideration to be given to a matter seemingly definitively settled. He wanted a change in a particular phrase. The congregation agreed to the move, and what originally read "human liberation" in the eleventh paragraph became the present "total and integral liberation of man, leading to participation in the life of God himself." Originally the congregation had voted that the official language of the declaration was to be the English in which the document had been written. It did so in part precisely because of the vigor with which that language had captured what the congregation wanted to say. Another intercession asked that the official text be the Latin version, with the English the original text for reference in making translations. The declaration lost much of that vigor in the rather orotund Latin; but since a Latin version was hardly what Jesuits and others were going to read and make use of practically, and since the delegates continued to be conciliatory and by now were in no mood to spend much time on such matters, they accepted the intercession on March 6, the second-last day of the congregation. The preparation and acceptance of this declaration was, in the minds of the delegates, one of the most encouraging and happiest outcomes of the congregation.

Who and When, Long or Short, Large or Small, Few or Many

Experience had by now taught the delegates about some of the problems to be encountered in general congregations and about some of the opportunities to be provided for province congregations. The preparatory commissions had produced studies that were thoughtful, detailed, and comprehensive. Most of the delegates had plenty of ideas and suggestions about what ought to be done to improve future general congregations; as the months rolled by and the present meeting continued, they had not been hesitant to express those ideas. But now when it came to agreeing on specific changes and doing anything about what they had experienced, the members of this congregation were at best only partly successful. A series of interlocking values was at stake. To enhance one of them often meant to diminish another. In several instances of proposals for improving a general congregation, this particular congregation could bring itself to the moment of choice but then could not choose. In other instances of such proposals, those pertaining to provincial congregations, it chose decisively and provided brilliantly for them.

General Congregations

On February 10 the delegate responsible for the section of the commission on governance that dealt with general congregations introduced to the assembly the report that would be the basis for several weeks of intermittent discussion and work. Intermittent, to be sure, because at the same time all of the events recounted in the immediately previous section of this history were also taking place. This text was at one and the same time an analysis of the experience of past and present congregations and a description of the ways in which each of the elements of a general congregation was usually linked with all the others. It also took into account that while the purpose of a general congregation was first and foremost legislative governance (for no other group in the Society could legislate for the whole Society), still the achievement of efficiency in coming to certain legislative goals had to be put into a context of purposes wider than the simple legislation itself. For example, one wider purpose of a congregation was to foster union among Jesuits. To confirm that, one need only note that the material on general congregations was contained in that part of the Constitutions of the Society that treated the unity of the Society.[68]

The commission proposed four possible areas of reform that the congregation might wish to consider. The first provided for thorough and "official" preparatory work antecedent to a general congregation itself. Such preparation would include the drafting of preliminary reports or *relationes præviæ*. Reports of that kind had been prepared for the present congregation, but they were not "official" in the technical juridical sense. So the present commissions of the congregation had in some instances almost reinvented the

---

[68] *Cons,* [655–718]: Part VIII, "Helps toward Uniting the Distant Members with Their Head and among Themselves."

wheel, writing all over again their own reports which did little to advance beyond what had already been prepared.

The second possible reform dealt with the number and type of participants in a general congregation. The topics raised here proved to be the most intractable when it came down to making any decisions about them. Should the by now traditional proportion of one-third ex officio delegates and two-thirds elected delegates continue to be the norm?[69] Should provincials attend only if elected? This roused the opposition of the provincials; they maintained that they had to attend if they were to implement back home in their provinces the decrees of a congregation. On the other hand, provincials cannot implement decrees quickly; and before they can accomplish this, within two years of a congregation's completion, from one-third to one-half of the provincials who attended the congregation will have been replaced. Should all provinces and vice-provinces have the same number of representatives, or at least should there be a better apportionment of representation? For example, in the present congregation some vice-provinces with one delegate had more than twice the number of Jesuit members as provinces with three delegates. In some instances the disparity was glaringly obvious. How large or small should a congregation be? The suggestions had ranged from the present size down to one of somewhere between 100 and 125 members. A problem here, of course, was that any increase in the number of provinces would increase the number of delegates even beyond the present size. Recent history had given little indication that the number of provinces could easily be reduced. There were any number of reasons for reducing the size of a congregation, from simple consideration of space—the present *aula* or congregation hall could hardly accommodate many more members—to complex considerations of how best to employ the talents of several hundred Jesuits over an extended period of time.

Time was the common denominator of the third question. How often should general congregations meet? Should they be on a regular, periodic schedule, say every six or nine years? At one time the Holy See had imposed on the Society the regulation that general congregations should meet at intervals of no more than nine years. On the other hand, that decision had followed on a very long period when no congregation had been held; and, as a matter of fact, the average interval at which congregations had been held in the history of the Society was not many years beyond nine. No matter when it met, how long should a congregation meet? The Thirty-second Congregation was experiencing vividly a long, long meeting. Should it meet for a fixed time, which only a two-thirds vote of the delegates could extend, or, as at present, without limit—described by one delegate as "interminably"? The fourth area of possible reform dealt with the types of general congregations. Might there be a congregation,

---

[69] Contrary to common opinion, this was not mandated by current legislation.

numerically small, with a mandate only to handle the kind of business which a congregation alone can deal with, and a numerically large congregation, such as the present one, called both for business and for the most important task of all, to elect a general?

The preliminary vote on whether to take up a matter that might "touch" the Constitutions passed easily. Then the customary assistancy groups met to discuss the report, and later on that same afternoon all met again in a general session.

On some points there was widespread agreement. For example, the proposal for improvements in procedure was happily received. For weeks delegates had been saying that weariness came not so much from too much work but from frustration at an overly rigid structure. The call for a thorough recasting of the *Formula of a General Congregation* was insistent. There was increasing recognition, too, that official preparation of first reports even before the congregation began could have obviated the redoing of so much at the beginning of the meeting. In general, the delegates were inclined to a flexible time limit for a congregation, although no one yet could describe what that meant. There was considerable doubt about not requiring the presence of all provincials. No one opposed the usefulness of cutting down the size of a general congregation; every specific proposal was opposed for one reason or another. At the end of the discussion, the drafting committee asked for written comments and suggestions as soon as possible and for replies to a questionnaire that would attempt to ascertain the directions to be followed in the work of proposing reforms.

Province Congregations

Meanwhile, the work of the subcommission on province congregations was proceeding apace. As had been noted earlier, a group of definitors had been elected to deal with the greater part of the detailed material on the subject, but the general congregation had reserved for its own deliberation and decision the question of enlarging participation in that province gathering. Fifty-eight postulata from the provinces had dealt with opening up to a greater number of Jesuits the possibility of participation in province congregations. A long discussion took place, in part about who should participate in a province congregation and in greater part about when he should participate, that is, after how many years as a member of the Society. At times an uninitiated newcomer at the meeting might have perceived resemblances between that discussion and the subsequent voting and an auction or a bingo game, as one number countered another. Should a Jesuit as yet without final vows be able to vote for province-congregation delegates after 2 or 10 years, after 3 or 8 years, after 4 or 7 years in the Society? Could someone be voted for after 5 or 10 years, after 6 or 9 years, after 7 years, after 8 years as a Jesuit? How many members without final vows might be delegates? Were 10 better than 15? Were 20 better than 5? A straw vote took place on February 24 on much of this material.

The commission prepared a simplified text. On February 28 a definitive vote was taken on this most important measure to increase participation in a province congregation by admitting delegates thereunto who did not yet have final vows, just as the Thirty-first General Congregation had introduced delegates other than the professed. Now more of the Jesuits would be involved in these most important official gatherings, at which their lives and activities came up for debate and elicited recommendations and prescriptions. The congregation decided that Jesuits not yet with final vows would under certain conditions enjoy the same rights to vote and be voted for in a province congregation as the Jesuits who already did have such vows. The conditions were as follows: One had the right to vote five years after entering the Society, and the right to be voted for eight years after entering. There could be no more than five such members in a province congregation and no more than three in a congregation of a vice-province. In every instance there had to be at least one such member. One proposal rejected by the congregation was for certain provinces to have those not yet in final vows make up a voting group separate and distinct from the rest of the province. Some postulata had favored participation in province congregations by Jesuits who were bishops, election by age groups, an order of preference in voting, and publication of the numerical results of the province election. None of these proposals was adopted. The General received the authority to revise in detail the *Formula of the Provincial Congregation* in accord with the decisions made here and, as was traditional, with the deliberative vote of members of the Jesuit curia who had an ex officio right to be present at a general congregation.

Decisions and Deferrals

To return to the material on a general congregation itself, the results of the questionnaire indicated, sometimes by small majorities, the following guidelines for further work: The *Formula* (or rules of procedure) *for a General Congregation* was to be rewritten in the sections that dealt with expediting business. Official and authoritative preparation would precede future meetings. congregations of procurators and of provincials could be given greater authority, for example, to write a report on the state of the Society or to suspend decrees of the preceding general congregation until the next one could review them. The number of elected delegates was to remain at least a majority but not necessarily two-thirds. Attendance by all provincials ex officio was to be maintained. Reduction of the number of delegates to about 180 was called for, but with a further report on this matter to the full assembly. There were no mandates for periodic and regularly scheduled congregations, for an antecedent limit on the length of a congregation, or for a double type of general congregation.

Eventually the decree that was passed included most of these provisions either in detail or in the form of a commission given to the General to see to their insertion in a revised *Formula of a General Congregation.*[70] The decree also permitted procurators "ad negotia" who were attending a general congregation to be elected to certain of its offices.

The one part of this reform material which on its very last day the congregation refused to deal with was the reduction in the number of delegates. Despite earlier and repeated determination to do something about it, despite the positive indications from the questionnaire, and despite a slender majority indicating tentative approval, the delegates were not willing to take decisive action. The topic was discussed with the utmost energy and at very great length. Every imaginable reason, pro and con, came to the floor, often with carefully modulated eloquence but deeply felt ardor. To cite but two examples: On the one hand the great debt that the Society owed to ancient provinces, generous and distinguished but now numerically small, was vividly described. No one, surely, would wish to reduce the number of delegates from such provinces that had for so long deserved so well of the Society! On the other hand, the glaring disparities in the number of Jesuits represented by delegates from different provinces were depicted with equal vividness. No one, surely, would wish to talk of justice in the world without considering the implications of justice in a matter so intimate to the Society itself! One of the delegates remarked in frustrated resignation that getting the congregation to take action in the matter of numbers was just about as easy as doing long division with Roman numerals.

Finally, on the question of reducing the number of participants in a general congregation, this Thirty-second Congregation wished also to do nothing. On March 7, the last day of the congregation, it voted to recommend to the General that he set up yet another commission to study the matter in greater depth in expectation that the Thirty-third Congregation would act upon it. Especially to be considered was how to stabilize or reduce the number of delegates, and how to set not only quantitative but also qualitative criteria in apportioning the numbers. No one seemed to know what qualitative criteria really meant.

On province congregations the delegates had acted carefully and forcefully. They adopted measures that brought about a more satisfactory participation by members of the Society, thus continuing the work of the Thirty-first Congregation. On general congregations, on the other hand, they acted carefully but hesitantly. In some instances they carried forward the work

---

[70] GC 32, D. 13 [303–11].

of the preceding congregation. In one instance, experienced and recognized as of great importance, namely, that of the number of delegates, they did only what their predecessors had done, essentially nothing. Several reasons might account for the refusal to act. First, the matter was recognizably important, but it was not as obviously and immediately so as others upon which the congregation had spent itself with great devotion. One had only so much energy available. Then too, the Pope's interventions, which still seemed to most delegates inexplicable, nonetheless induced caution as they considered anything that might be construed as further fueling papal worries. Thirdly, although the matter of congregations was one of the priority items from the start of the meeting, many of the specific questions came up for discussion and decision only very late in the congregation. Next, the specific question of numbers of delegates involved the sensitivities and interests of a great many diverse groups, and the opportunity was lacking to bring them into active involvement early and then throughout the process of preparing concrete proposals. Finally, as students of organizational behavior regularly observe, self-reform is the most difficult task any deliberative assembly can undertake.

Conclusion

Full Circle

On February 25 the delegates had set March 8 as the last date for congregation sessions. In the interval there was much yet to do. Among the most important of those tasks was the completion of the document on the mission of the Society today. On February 21, a few days before the vote on the closing date, a fourth report and a new version of the text came from the joint drafting committee of the three commissions charged with the subject. It was the result of a huge number of suggestions occasioned by the previous version that had appeared earlier in the month in French, English, and Spanish. This fourth text enjoyed, if again that is the word, yet more amendments. They and the body of the text with even more amendments came to definitive and overwhelmingly positive votes on March 1 and 3. What had been the subject of strong reservations and intense debate and had seemed almost impossible back near the beginning of the congregation was now a reality, a decree on faith and justice enthusiastically accepted by the vast majority of the delegates. It clearly situated the service of the faith at the center of the apostolic work of the Society, while at the same time putting the promotion of justice as an absolute and inescapable requirement of that service.

Also among the pressing tasks was to see how well the congregation had been faithful to the mandates sent to it by fellow members of the Society and how well it had responded to the concerns voiced by the Holy See. In the former case, it had only to consider how it had responded to the postulata from fellow Jesuits. In the latter case, it had clear and sometimes conflicting indications. But it did have, most recently, the letter from the Pope summarizing those concerns in general.

In his February 15, 1975, letter to Fr. Arrupe, in response to the congregation's account of the reasons for dealing with the question of grades, Pope Paul VI had said, "Therefore, we repeat confidently the question which we asked in our address on the 3rd of December at the beginning of the congregation, 'Where are you going?'" and he asked the delegates to "consider seriously before the Lord the decisions to be made."[71] In response, the General with the assent of the congregation quickly named a special committee to look again at the texts of the documents which the congregation—as it neared the decisive voting stage—was preparing to approve and compare them with the papal address of December 3, 1974, with the letters that the Pope had sent after the beginning of the congregation, and with other recent papal pronouncements to and for the Society. The chairman of the committee, was Carlo Martini, the official liaison between the congregation and the papal secretariat of state. It had two other members, working with the four recently elected general assistants—with Paolo Dezza, recently retired as a general assistant, as a special consultant.[72] This task force was to prepare a list of the items to which the Pope had urged the congregation to address itself, to look at the work of the congregation and see if any items had perhaps not been dealt with, and, if so, to suggest ways in which to deal with them.

A week later, on February 24, the task force gave its first report to the delegates. It listed in detail the points that the Pope had considered of fundamental importance for the Society; it judged that almost all of them were to be found in the documents now in various stages of final preparation and in the documents of the Thirty-first Congregation to which the current texts made frequent reference, very often with the stated intent of confirming them. The task force thought, too, that the document "Jesuits Today," still in preparation, admirably and in an inspiring way stated the essentials of Jesuit life. It suggested, lastly, that a prefatory decree precede the collection of documents of the present congregation. That decree would explicitly confirm the Thirty-first Congregation, reaffirm the essential points about the Society that the Pope had emphasized, and introduce the decrees of the present congregation with an eye to putting them into practice. The task force had prepared an example of such a text. It occasioned much comment in assistancy meetings and in a plenary session, especially with reference to its second part on those essential points. A

---

[71] GC 32, Document III, p. 540.

[72] Fr. Dezza had for many years been a consultant to various Vatican offices. He was at this time also confessor to Pope Paul VI.

further report took shape, shorter and with a different version of that second section.

On March 5, now only two days before the end, the congregation voted to have an "introductory decree," to use this further report as its basis, to have it revised and amended, and to consider it once more in final form. On March 7 the revised and amended text was voted in during the second session of that last day. It spoke of the success of the efforts to implement the work of the previous congregation, said as clearly as possible that it "makes its own and confirms all of the declarations and dispositions of the Thirty-first General Congregation," and affirmed that those documents "accurately and faithfully express the genuine spirit and tradition of the Society."[73] The decree recognized, secondly, that progress had not been uniform, described the reasons for that, gave examples of problems, pointed to the concerns of the Pope, acknowledged failings, and recalled that "it was to a balanced renewal of religious life and a discerning rededication to apostolic service"[74] that both the Pope and the General had called the Society. Lastly, it stated the purpose of the present decrees as "an invitation to even greater progress in the way of the Lord,"[75] pointed out that they looked "far beyond words and verbal analysis," and were "offered as a stimulus for conversion of hearts and apostolic renewal."[76]

As were the last weeks, so was the last day of the congregation very busy. During the morning of March 7, the General and the four general assistants left the session for several hours to go to an audience with the Pope at which he gave a farewell address for the congregation.[77] On their return, the General and the assistants came into the *aula* as the congregation was in session, one of the assistants carrying in a large dark-green velvet brass-bound antique case, a gift from the Pope to the General for the congregation. The General read to the delegates the Pope's address. Concluding with an observation on how important were the tasks of the Society and how the eyes of contemporary men, of members of other religious orders, and of the universal Church were turned toward the Society, it voiced the wish that such grandly conceived hopes would not be frustrated.

Speculation was abundantly imaginative as to the contents of the case. After reading the address, the General opened it and presented the gift. It was the seventeenth-century crucifix which had been the personal possession of the great Jesuit theologian and ardent defender of the Holy See, St. Robert (Cardi-

---

[73] GC 32, D. 1:2 [2].

[74] Ibid., 1:5 [5].

[75] Ibid., 1:5 [7].

[76] Ibid., 1:9 [9].

[77] Ibid., Document IV, Address of Pope Paul VI in the Presence of Father General and the General Assistants, March 7, 1975.

nal) Bellarmine. The symbolism was clear and clearly had been known and intended. But as some informally noted later when they had reflected on Bellarmine's life, loyalty to and defense of the Holy See was only the immediately obvious message. Robert Bellarmine had indeed loved and defended the popes of his time. He had also modestly but quite directly told them the truth as he saw it, had pointed out to Sixtus V the clear errors in the Pope's editing of the Vulgate, had at one time been temporarily sent by Clement VIII into honorable exile as an archbishop, and had written respectfully but frankly to Paul V about how not to go about deciding the long-controverted question of grace and the helps thereunto. Bellarmine had propounded the theological theory of the indirect temporal power of the papacy; and the Holy See had come close to publicly condemning his teaching as erroneous and putting the book containing it on the Index. Yet, in the twentieth century the Holy See used that theory as the accepted and approved doctrine; and for calling it into question John Courtney Murray was silenced, only to be vindicated by the Second Vatican Council itself, presided over by Paul VI. Symbols are rich. The Pope who presented the gift presumably knew that as well as anyone might.

Late in the afternoon of March 7, with every decree at last voted on, the congregation gave the General the usual powers to complete the details of its legislative work and the power to dissolve colleges and professed houses until the next congregation (a curious but necessary faculty because the Constitutions explicitly reserve that to a general congregation).[78] Fr. Arrupe addressed the delegates assembled for the last time. Then, as at the beginning they had in the Veni, Creator begged the Spirit's help, so now in gratitude for it they prayed the Te Deum to close the congregation, Finally, for all the work of ninety-six days and eighty-three plenary sessions and more than thirteen hundred ballots, for uncounted committee meetings, for food and drink and light and heat and secretarial assistance, and for encouragement and friendship and prayers, the General invited in all the Jesuits, brothers and priests, who had helped the congregation in any way, to receive in the unity of one Society, the recognition and thanks of the delegates as they concluded a congregation that had surely been "more extraordinary than others."

The Congregation on Mission

However extraordinary the life and activities of this or any other general congregation might have been, the congregation was meant not for itself but for the ordinary life and activity of the Society of Jesus. Having come full circle from its beginning on Dec. 2, 1974, to its conclusion on March 7, 1975, as a congregation of the Society of Jesus it ceased to exist except in Jesuit history, but as an influence on the Society it had just begun.

[78] *Cons,* [322, 441, 680, 763].

The elements of the congregation that would influence the Society for almost the next twenty years Fr. Arrupe succinctly and accurately summarized in his letter to the whole Society on putting into effect the decrees of the congregation. Noting that throughout the documents several concepts repeatedly stood out, he asked that they be the touchstone to which efforts at implementation regularly return. They are the concepts of mission, of incarnation in human realities (this includes "inculturation"), of integration in apostolates, in formation, in cooperation among provinces, of union of minds and hearts, of community of friends in the Lord, of authority as service, of poverty, and of humble and open collaboration.[79]

But the term "Full Circle," employed as a title for the immediately preceding section of this study, can be attached to more than simply the period of the congregation itself. That gathering also came full circle in complementing and completing the work of its predecessor, the Thirty-first Congregation. Together they constituted a remarkable program for the renewal of the Society of Jesus in accord with the mind of the Church as expressed most authoritatively in the Second Vatican Council. Together they developed the principles for the program of adaptation and renovation that the Thirty-first Congregation decisively chose in the following statement:

> Thus it has determined that the entire government of the Society must be adapted to modern necessities and ways of living; that our whole training in spirituality and in studies must be changed; that religious and apostolic life itself is to be renewed; that our ministries are to be weighed in relation to the pastoral spirit of the Council according to the criterion of the greater and more universal service of God in the modern world; and that the very spiritual heritage of our Institute, containing both new and old elements, is to be purified and enriched anew according to the necessities of our times.[80]

The congregation came full circle in an even wider perspective. Much of the contemporaneity, imagination, and daring of the early years of the Society had inevitably been lost in the wrack and ruin of the Suppression in 1773. In theory it might have been possible to restore that freshness at the Restoration in 1814. Despite all the fidelity, zeal, and goodwill that existed then and later, such was not to be. For a great number of reasons, some internal to the Society, some internal to the Church, some external to both, that freshness did not break forth again with the Restoration of the Society nor did it appear in the following decades. Then Vatican II came upon the Church and unshackled possibilities in world and Church and in the Society of Jesus too. The Thirty-second General Congregation, in combination with its predecessor, gave

---

[79] *AR* 16 (1976): 544–48, Letter to the Whole Society concerning the Implementation of the Decrees of General Congregation 32.

[80] GC 31, D. 2:1 [211].

to Jesuits, individually and collectively, the opportunity to return full circle and in contemporary ways back to the élan and imagination of the early Society and of the service it gave to the Church.

That return points up, too, how radically conservative the congregation was. It had its roots in the fundamental spirit of the Society, in the charism of its founder, in the attitudes that pervade the Spiritual Exercises. It was conservative, too, in that it drew from the members of the Society itself the programs which they, through preparations and postulata and province congregations, had requested of the congregation. Finally, and perhaps paradoxically, this and the preceding Thirty-first Congregation were conservative in being open to the future in a way that for the first time was reminiscent of the founding years of the Society.

All of this return to sources that make possible an openness to the future may have been too much to institutionalize adequately in the work and documents of the congregation; surely the structures needed to carry out the decisions of the congregation in the everyday life of the Society are still, even now, in process of formation.

In so many thousands of words, the Thirty-second Congregation had tried to witness to and express the contemporary apostolic mission of the Society and the Jesuit life consequent upon it. Now the hope of their fulfillment had to rest on the Lord and on those who would follow him and witness to him in the community of the Church and in the fellowship of the Society of Jesus. As the delegates prepared to leave Rome, there was an ever recurrent symbol for that hope. On ground where, it is said, early Christian martyrs had once witnessed to the faith, within sight of St. Peter's, watched over by the heroic-sized statue of Jesus Christ, in the garden of the curia of the Society of Jesus the first flowers of spring had opened wide.

GENERAL CONGREGATION 33

Note

The events of the two years that led up to the Thirty-third General Congregation were so unusual and the congregation itself was so recent that at present it would be difficult to write even a brief history of that meeting.

The events themselves included the stroke that felled Fr. General Pedro Arrupe in August 1981; the appointment in October of Fr. Paolo Dezza as the Pope's delegate, with Fr. Giuseppe Pittau as the delegate's coadjutor, to govern the Society and to prepare for the congregation; the meeting of all the Jesuit provincials in Rome in February 1982; and finally in December of that year the delegate's summoning of the congregation to begin in September 1983. So extraordinary were several of those events, so deeply were they felt in the Society, and so recent has the congregation itself been that it would be difficult at present to write a real history that would maintain a proper and historically objective distance from the events and from the participants, known and yet to be known, that were involved.

What follows, therefore, in this part of the present book, is simply the Historical Preface to the decrees of the Thirty-third General Congregation in an authorized English translation from the official Latin text. It appears on pages 13 to 38 of the volume Documents of the Thirty-Third General Congregation of the Society of Jesus, *edited by Donald R. Campion, S.J., and Albert C. Louapre, S.J., and published by the Institute of Jesuit Sources, St. Louis, in 1984. For the sake of uniformity, some comparatively minor stylistic changes have been introduced into this official translation.*

John W. Padberg, S.J.

Historical Preface

1. Prior to Convocation

As far back as 1980 Very Reverend Father General Pedro Arrupe had in mind the summoning of a general congregation to which, after the votes of the provincials had been secured, he would submit his resignation from the office of Superior General. The Supreme Pontiff John Paul II, however, asked Father General to postpone this step so that the Society might prepare itself more profoundly for a congregation.[1] The following year, after a grave illness unexpectedly befell Father General on August 7,[2] the Supreme Pontiff in a letter dated October 5[3] named Father Paolo Dezza (Italy) as his Delegate in charge of seeing to the preparation of the Society for the general congregation and the temporary government of the Society. He also named Father Giuseppe Pittau (Japan) to be the Delegate's coadjutor.

On February 27, 1982, the Supreme Pontiff addressed the provincials of the Society, who had met together with Father Delegate in Villa Cavalletti, concerning his desires with respect to the Society and to the preparation of the congregation, and at the same time expressed his confidence that the convocation itself could occur before the year's end.[4] This, in fact, came about when, on December 8, 1982, Father Delegate, with the permission of the Supreme Pontiff, summoned the general congregation for September 1, 1983. "The task of General Congregation XXXIII will be first of all to deal with the resignation of Father General and the election of a new General; then it will be to treat of those matters which are to be reviewed in accord with the will of the Holy See (cf. Cardinal Villot's letter of May 2, 1975) and of General Congregation XXXII; and finally, as the general congregation itself judges best, it will treat the postulates sent to the general congregation."[5] Father Delegate asked that the province congregations be completed by April 10, 1983.

2. The Official Preparatory Committee Is Established

After the province congregations were completed, Father Delegate promptly established the "Official Preparatory Committee" (in accordance with the Formula of the General Congregation 12, #1), which was being put to use for the first time. Those named to this committee from each of the assistancies were Fathers Albert Beaudry (English), Michel Chu (East Asian), James A. Devereux (American), Julian Fernandes (Indian), Claude Flipo (French), Johannes G. Gerhartz (German), João MacDowell (Southern Latin American), Daniel Pasupasu (African), Zygmunt Perz (Slavic), Roberto Tucci (Italian), Urbano Valero (Spanish), and Jesús Vergara (Northern Latin American). It was the task of the Official Preparatory Committee, according to the norms of the Formula of the General Congregation, "to complete the proximate preparation" (12, #1), and to do that in an "authoritative" manner in the sense that the studies and reports produced or approved by it "should be regarded as part of the official

---

[1] *Acta Romana* 18:225 (Letter of July 3, 1980). Hereafter the *Acta Romana* will be cited as *AR*.

[2] *AR* 18:608ff.

[3] *AR* 18:401.

[4] *AR* 18:721–34.

[5] *AR* 18:856–58.

work of the congregation and acknowledged by the congregation itself" (10, #2, 2°).

3. The Work of the Official Preparatory Committee

The Preparatory Committee convened in Rome at the general curia on June 1, 1983, and carried on its efforts up to the end of the month. It undertook first, in accordance with the norm of the Formula of the General Congregation 13, its duty of screening the postulates and in doing so examined all those sent by the province congregations and those that individuals had sent within the prescribed time. It drew up a report on the postulates admitted for handling in the general congregation or given to Father General or rejected.

Next it prepared necessary preliminary reports. Three of these dealt with points that a future congregation would have to handle by wish of the Holy See (cf. letter of Cardinal Villot, May 2, 1975) and of the Thirty-second General Congregation, namely, the question of confirmation of Decree 12 of the Thirty-second General Congregation with respect to poverty, and certain questions about participation in a province congregation and about the makeup of a general congregation.

The other preliminary reports prepared by the Official Preparatory Committee had to do with our apostolic mission (with questions about the confirmation and clarification of Decree 4 of the Thirty-second General Congregation, and about some of its applications, especially concerning the promotion of peace and international order, about collaboration with lay persons, about the apostolate of education, and about some other types of apostolate), with the coadjutor brothers, with religious life, with the formation of Jesuits, with the relationship of the Society to the hierarchical Church. On all these topics, moreover, drafts of statements that might be useful for discussion in the general congregation were prepared.

At the conclusion of these efforts, in early July, Father Delegate sent an announcement to all those who were to attend the congregation in order to inform them about the main points handled by the Preparatory Committee. The preliminary reports themselves, along with the postulates assembled by categories and a report on the postulates, were handed to all who were to attend the congregation the day they reached Rome for the general congregation. They were able to apply themselves to the study of these materials from the start of the congregation, that is, even before the election of the Superior General.

4. The Members of the Congregation Convene

On the prescribed day almost all those who were to participate in the congregation were on hand in Rome at the general curia and the adjoining House of Writers. Still, a few were missing. Because of circumstances a province congregation could not be held in Bohemia, Hungary, Lithuania, Romania, and Slovakia. From Hungary only the provincial came, but he was joined by another member of the same province (but living outside its territory) who was named by Father Delegate in accordance with the norm of the Formula of the Province Congregation 95, #4. For Bohemia, Lithuania, and Slovakia, Father Delegate, in accordance with the norm of the Formula of the Province Congregation 95, #3, named as members three Jesuits living outside their native countries. But no one came on behalf of Romania. During the first days of the congregation, Father Joseph Labaj (provincial of Wisconsin) was absent because of illness. He came afterwards and took part in the election of Father General and of the general assistants. On September 23, however, he had to take permanent leave of the congregation.

5. Concelebration with Pope John Paul II

On the first day of the congregation, September 2, which was the first Friday of the month, the Supreme Pontiff John Paul II wished to come from Castel Gandolfo to our curia in order that he might concelebrate the Eucharistic liturgy with the members of the congregation and address them in a homily. After the liturgy was concluded, in a further demonstration of exceptional goodwill, of his own accord he also stayed on to visit with the members of the congregation and to speak familiarly with each of them.

6. First Session of the Congregation

(From the Minutes, Acta 1)

In the afternoon of the same day, the first session was held. After the singing of the hymn *Veni Creator Spiritus* and a brief greeting delivered to the members by Father Delegate, the congregation was declared to be fully and legitimately in session. Then the congregation had put before it the case of the four electors from France and the five from Italy, called on behalf of each of the vice-provinces that exist in these large provinces, in accordance with the statutes set down by Father General (*AR* 16:749 and *AR* 17:359). When this decision was ratified, the nine electors were summoned to the *aula*. The congregation also decreed the admission, as observers in these first sessions, but excluding the session of the election, [of] those members who had the right to participate only in matters of business and likewise [of] Father Donald Campion (New York), the director of the Information Office.

Next, approval was given to the "Additions" on procedure proposed by Father Delegate, as well as norms on information that he presented. Approval was given likewise to the creation, proposed by Father Delegate, of a committee to supervise the communication of information. This committee was made up of Fathers Marcello Azevedo (Central East Brazil), Joaquin G. Bernas (Philippines), Andre Costes (France), Federico Lombardi (Italy), Fernando Montes (Chile), Stanislaw Opiela (Greater Poland), Vitus Seibel (Upper Germany), and Urbano Valero (Castile).

7. Acceptance of Very Reverend Father Arrupe's Resignation

(From the Minutes, Acta 2, 3)

On September 3, after the election of Father M. Azevedo (Central East Brazil) as secretary of the congregation for the election and of Father J. Gerhartz (Northern Germany) as his assistant, the congregation dealt with the question of accepting or not accepting the resignation of Very Reverend Father Pedro Arrupe. After a brief discussion this resignation was accepted by a secret vote. A special solemn session, at which were present also members of the curia community and all the other Jesuit houses in Rome, was held in the afternoon of the same day, in order to manifest the Society's gratitude to Very Reverend Father Arrupe, just as different postulates from province congregations expressly requested. Father Delegate delivered an address in which he recalled the examples given us all by Father Arrupe, his total dedication to his office and his ardent love for the Society and every one of its members, and the unflagging inspiration he gave to the Society in its effort to adapt itself according to its own spirit to new circumstances and needs. Finally, Father Delegate stressed the new model of abnegation set before all by Father Arrupe in these last years, namely, when he wanted to put into action the procedure authorized by the Thirty-first General Congregation for resigning from his office, but had to postpone his resignation and was subsequently struck by illness.

After thunderously protracted applause, Father Ignacio Iglesias (Leon), a member of the congregation, read the text of a message to the Society drafted by Father Arrupe with the help of the General Assistants. This memorable session was brought to a close with a reception in the curia garden. On the next day, which was a Sunday, a Eucharistic liturgy was concelebrated in the cathedral at La Storta with Father Arrupe, who also visited the nearby chapel that had recently been restored in accordance with his wish. A homily prepared by Father Arrupe was read by Father Juan Luis Fernández-Castañeda (Peru) and the consecration of the Society to the Sacred Heart of Jesus was renewed according to a text edited by Father Arrupe some years ago.

8. Election of the Deputation on the State of the Society

(From the Minutes, Acta 4)

On the morning of September 4[*] those fathers were elected who would form the deputation on the state of the Society together with Father Delegate and his coadjutor and the four general assistants (Jean-Yves Calvez, Parmananda Divarkar, Cecil McGarry, Vincent O'Keefe): Philibert Randriambololona (for the African Assistancy), John O'Callaghan (American Assistancy), Juan Ochagavia (Southern Latin American), Carlos Soltero (Northern Latin American), Michael Campbell-Johnston (English), Robert Rush (East Asian), Denis Delobre (French), Eugen Hillengass (German), Ignacio Iglesias (Spanish), Michael Amaladoss (Indian), Bruno Bois (Italian), Zygmunt Perz (Slavic). When Fathers Amaladoss, O'Callaghan and Ochagavia subsequently were elected general assistants, the congregation elected three others as their substitutes: Fathers Parmananda Divarkar, Joseph O'Hare, and Manuel Guttierrez Semprun, in accordance with the norms of the Formula of the General Congregation 100, #2.

After the election of the deputies it was announced that the time set for presenting information to the deputation was a period of two days, i.e., up to and including September 6. Information was given also about the list of judges concerning "ambition" in accordance with the norm of the Formula of the General Congregation 54.

9. Report of Father Delegate and the Four Days for Gathering Information

(From the Minutes, Acta 5, 8)

On September 5, Father Delegate made a report, in accordance with the spirit of the Formula of the General Congregation 37, on those things he had done from October 5, 1981, when the government of the Society was entrusted to him. On the following day, he replied to the written observations and questions that had been handed in by members of the congregation. On September 8, 1983, the report on the state of the Society drafted by the deputation was distributed. The congregation decreed that the quatriduum for gathering information in preparation for the election of the superior general should begin on September 9. On the following day, Father Delegate reminded all of the special duty of recollection and he also stressed the importance of our rules for the giving and receiving of information on an individual basis, which forbid

---

[*] [There seems to be a mistake in the dating here. If Fr. Arrupe resigned on September 3 and "on the next day (September 4), which was a Sunday," the celebration took place at La Storta, then "on the morning of September 4" the congregation could not have elected the deputation on the state of the Society. ED.]

everything that could have even the appearance of any kind of propaganda. In fact, an atmosphere of deep recollection, prayer, and spiritual discernment flourished during these four days, an experience that was praised by all the electors.

10. Election of the Superior General

(From the Minutes, Acta 9)

After the completion of the quatriduum, on the morning of September 13, all the members of the congregation, with Father Delegate as presiding celebrant, concelebrated the Mass of the Holy Spirit. At the conclusion of the sacred liturgy, the electors went immediately to the *aula* of the congregation where, in accordance with the Formula, they were enclosed. When the hymn *Veni Creator* was said, Father Edward Sheridan (Upper Canada), the speaker duly designated for the occasion, gave a fifteen-minute exhortation to the electors, in accordance with the prescription of the Formula of the General Congregation 75, #1 "for the election of a Superior who would be best suited for the greater service of God." After that, all prayed for the rest of the hour.

Then, after all the prescriptions of the Formula were fulfilled, by majority vote on the first ballot Father Peter-Hans Kolvenbach of the Vice-province of the Near East, was elected superior general of the Society. He had been formerly provincial of this vice-province and for almost two years was serving as rector of the Pontifical Oriental Institute in Rome. The formal certification of this election was drawn up immediately and signed by Father Delegate. The news was sent to the Supreme Pontiff, who was in Austria engaged in an apostolic journey.

In remarks he delivered immediately after the election, the new superior general made plain again the Society's enormous gratitude toward Father Arrupe, and expressed the fullest thanks to Father Paolo Dezza for his work as the Pope's Delegate as well as to Father Giuseppe Pittau for the staunch assistance he rendered, and to the entire curia, but especially to the general assistants for the way in which they helped the entire Society in the last years.

Then Father Pedro Arrupe came into the *aula* and greeted with heartfelt warmth his successor as Superior General of the Society. All then moved on to the curia chapel to give thanks to God with a *Te Deum.*

11. Election of the Secretary and Sub-Secretaries and Likewise of the Deputation for Handling Substantive Matters

(From the Minutes, Acta 10)

After the election of the Superior General, on September 15 Father Johannes Gunter Gerhartz (Northern Germany) was elected secretary for the further work of the congregation, i.e., for substantive matters. Fathers Simon Decloux (Southern Belgium) and Jean-Yves Calvez (France) were elected as sub-secretaries. The deputation for handling substantive matters was also established immediately and the following were elected to it: Fathers Daniel Pasupasu (for the African Assistancy), Vincent O'Keefe (American), João MacDowell (Southern Latin American), Cesar Jerez (Northern Latin American), Cecil McGarry (English), Giuseppe Pittau (East Asian), Henri Madelin (French), Hans van Leeuwen (Netherlands), Urbano Valero (Spanish), Abraham Puthumana (Indian), Roberto Tucci (Italian), and Petar Galauner (Slavic).

A small committee within this deputation was elected to assist in handling the daily problems concerning the order of treatment of topics (cf. Formula of the General Congregation 101, #6). The members of this committee were Fathers Henri Madelin, Vincent O'Keefe, and Roberto Tucci. The latter two along with Father Simon Decloux were named by Father General as moderators of the various sessions (in accordance with the norm of the Formula of the General Congregation 101, #7).

12. Reports on the Work Rendered by the Preparatory Committee. Setting Up of Commissions

(From the Minutes, Acta 11, 12, 13, 14)

In accordance with a decision made on September 16, the quatriduum prior to the election of the general assistants began on the following day, i.e., September 17. During the period of the quatriduum, however, the first steps were taken with respect to handling substantive matters. On the one hand, preliminary reports of the Official Preparatory Committee on the province congregation and on coadjutor brothers were presented in the *aula*. On the other hand, the congregation entrusted the setting up of commissions on handling substantive matters to Father General together with the deputation on handling substantive matters. Eight commissions were immediately set up: On Poverty (Moderator: Father Eugen Hillengass); On the Province Congregation (Moderator: Father Stefan Bamberger); On the General Congregation (Moderator: Father Jean-Yves Calvez); On Our Mission (Moderator: Father Juan Ochagavia, who was replaced by Father William Ryan when he was later elected a general assistant); On the Relationship of the Society to the Church and Its Hierarchy (Moderator: Father Theodor Beirle); On Coadjutor Brothers (Moderator: Father Claude Flipo); On Religious Life (Moderator: Father Rex

Pai); On Jesuit Formation (Moderator: Father Michael Amaladoss). Each commission had twelve members, one from each assistancy, except, however, for the Commission on Our Mission, which had two members from each Assistancy.

After a few days a judicial committee was established, made up of three members, namely, Fathers Antonio Arza (Loyola), Francisco Egaña (Loyola) and Ladislas Orsy (New York). In the final days of the congregation, a small special commission was set up to handle a certain postulate concerning the law of the Society on parishes.

13. Election of General Assistants and Admonitor and Appointment of General Counsellors and Certain Regional Assistants

(From the Mintues, Acta 15, 16, 17, 20)

The election of the general assistants was held, in accordance with the norm of the Formula of the General Congregation 136, #2, in three different sessions. In the first, on September 21, two were elected; in the second, in the afternoon of the same day, one; in the third, on September 22, one. Those elected were Father Michael Amaladoss, from the Province of Madurai; Father Simon Decloux, from the Province of Southern Belgium; Father John J. O'Callaghan, from the Province of Chicago; Father Juan Ochagavia, from the Province of Chile.

By the fact of their election the four general assistants became also general counsellors. Father General afterwards, with a deliberative vote of the general assistants, named two other general counselors: Father Giuseppe Pittau (Japan), who most recently functioned as coadjutor to the Pope's Delegate, and Urbano Valero (Castile), who hitherto was rector of the Pontifical University of Comillas. Father Simon Decloux (Southern Belgium) was elected admonitor of the Superior General on September 24.

During the course of the congregation, some regional assistants also were appointed: for the American Assistancy, Father Joseph Whelan, hitherto provincial of the Province of Maryland; for the East Asian Assistancy and at the same time for the Italian Assistancy, Father Giuseppe Pittau, already appointed as a general counselor; for the French Assistancy, Father Simon Decloux, already elected as general assistant, general counselor and admonitor; for the Spanish Assistancy, Father Urbano Valero, already appointed as general counselor; for the Indian Assistancy, Father Noel D'Souza (Calcutta), hitherto rector of the Jesuit theologate in Pune; for the Slavic Assistancy, Father Andrzej Koprowski (Greater Poland), hitherto rector of the Jesuit theologate in Warsaw.

14. Method of Handling Substantive Matters

(From the Minutes, Acta 27, 30)

The process followed in handling substantive matters in this congregation was most frequently the same: an oral presentation of a preliminary report *(relatio prævia)* drafted by the Official Preparatory Committee; meetings of Assistancy groups for the purpose of preparing written comments; a revised report *(relatio secunda)* prepared by a commission (with a presentation of the comments received, a judgment of the commission, and a draft of a decree or declaration to be issued by the congregation); a brief oral presentation of the revised report with an opportunity to pose questions for the sake of clarification and the debate itself in the *aula* (without any previous consideration in small groups); presentation of amendments and a final vote on them and on the body of the text. In certain cases, however, the text, after the debate in the *aula*, would have to be rewritten by the commission again and an opportunity found for a new presentation and debate.

Still, it soon became evident that a wish existed in the congregation to have all those elements that could be said to be rather orientative and inspirational in nature woven together and unified in a single document that would reveal to all the members of the Society the congregation's own thinking on both our mission and our life. Nevertheless, it seemed good not to make a decision in this matter too quickly in order to avoid hindering the work of the individual commissions and the serious treatment of each theme.

After a discussion on the matter in a plenary session on October 6, the congregation determined to attempt the drafting of one document that would bring together the texts prepared by individual commissions, after they were debated in the *aula* but prior to the final process of amendments. Amendments, therefore, properly speaking, were made with respect to a document already unified by a certain editorial committee. This committee was empowered to eliminate repetitions and as far as possible unify the style. The editorial committee set up on October 11 included Fathers Albert Beaudry (French Canada), Ignacio Iglesias (León), and Joseph O'Hare (New York).

This is the genesis of the document "Companions of Jesus Sent into Today's World."[6] It was brought into the *aula* on October 18. At that time the first part, and later the second, was submitted for study to the assistancy groups, in which the majority of the amendments were prepared that were later brought forward in the *aula*. Voting on all amendments and on the entire document took place on October 24.

Beyond the single document there remained questions having to do with the province congregation and the general congregation as well as the

---

[6] D. I, see p. 41ff. below.

confirmation, in the proper sense of the word, of Decree 12 of the Thirty-second General Congregation concerning poverty.[7]

In the sections that follow, these three latter points are treated first, and then those contained in the "unique document" (Decree 1) in the order in which they are found in the document itself.

15. On the Province Congregation

(From the Minutes, Acta 13, 25)

The Thirty-first General Congregation instituted representation in the province congregation through a preliminary election, in which also spiritual coadjutors and coadjutor brothers, within certain limits, could be elected. The Thirty-second General Congregation, however, decreed some measure of participation also for those not yet with final vows,[8] but wished that the provisions thus set down should be reviewed by the next general congregation. In addition, the secretary of state, in a letter of May 2, 1975, asked for a review of the entire question by a future general congregation.[9]

The Thirty-third General Congregation was obliged, therefore, to examine the matter. A broad body of information was gathered from the provinces both through postulates and through replies to a document sent out by Father Delegate along with a letter of December 31, 1982.[10] After considering this information, the Preparatory Committee prepared a preliminary report which examined the whole issue, including the question of a preliminary election itself.

Then the commission and the congregation itself devoted like attention to all aspects of the question, including the problem of whether the limitation on the number of coadjutor brothers who are admitted to a province congregation should perhaps be lifted.

After study and debate, it was concluded, first, that the system of a preliminary election for forming a province congregation should be retained; but, second, that the norms set by the Thirty-second General Congregation on the participation of members without final vows should remain in force but should be reviewed again by the next general congregation. For it was seen, on the one hand, that the harmful effects which were feared had not arisen in the province congregations of 1978 and 1983, but rather that beneficial results with respect to union and integration have appeared and gravely harmful effects

---

[7] D. 2–6, see p. 65–73 below.

[8] GC 32, D. 14, n. 11.

[9] *AR* 16:461.

[10] *AR* 18:909ff.

certainly are not to be expected prior to the next general congregation. On the other hand, it was seen that the time for experimentation has not yet been sufficiently lengthy to permit a definitive judgment in the matter.[11]

With this conclusion reached, the congregation did not wish to decree anything about other points (e.g., concerning the limit on the participation of coadjutor brothers with final vows). For some of these points require deeper study, that must be made prior to the next congregation, on account of the connection with the priestly nature of the Society.

16. On the Composition of the General Congregation

(From the Minutes, Acts 19, 26, 28, 35)

With respect to the general congregation, the outstanding question concerned the composition and number of its members. The Thirty-first and Thirty-second General Congregations already had considered the problem but could not decide on a solution.[12] The Thirty-second Congregation, however, in its Decree 13, n. 7, recommended to the Superior General that he should set up a commission "to examine the following questions in more detail in preparation for their consideration and decision by the next general congregation:

- stabilizing the number of those who attend a general congregation
- apportioning the members of the general congregation according to criteria which are not only quantitative but also qualitative;
- reducing the numbers of those who attend a general congregation."

The commission was already set up in 1975. It included Fathers Johannes G. Gerhartz (Northern Germany) as chairman, and Jean-Yves Calvez (France), Paolo Dezza (Italy), Casimir Gnanadickam (Madurai), and William G. Guindon (New England). The commission conducted widespread consultations and presented three successive reports between 1976 and 1982. The third of these reports was sent to the province congregations prior to the Thirty-third General Congregation. After an analysis both of the unequal situations arising from the traditional system of representation in a general congregation and of difficulties coming from the great number of members of a congregation, the report proposed several solutions. All of them offered the possibility of greater proportionality, to the extent that small units (having their own characteristic experience) would send at least one elector and thus account would be taken of qualitative representation. Different solutions, however, offered different degrees of reduction of numbers (or at least numerical stabilization).

---

[11] See D. 5, p. 70 below.

[12] Cf. Historical Preface to the Decrees of GC 31, n. 31 (*AR* 14:836f.); Historical Preface to the Decrees of GC 32, n. 19 (*AR* 16:301f.).

If any of the solutions offered were to gain the consensus of the congregation, it would be possible to abolish the title of independent vice-province. The name province would be employed in future also for what are currently independent vice-provinces. For the sole difference with respect to an independent vice-province concerned participation in a general congregation.

All these proposals were endorsed by the Official Preparatory Committee, which introduced slight changes with regard both to restoring a slightly higher proportion of those sent by the provinces through election, and to a slightly greater favoring of the larger provinces. These changes were subsequently lessened by the commission in accordance with comments received.

A concern about the representation of different cultures and experiences, which had been manifested back in the Thirty-second General Congregation, surfaced again in this congregation. For the most part, however, it seemed that the proposed solutions answered this concern to a sufficient degree.

In another area, some difficulty seemed to be present in the fact that, according to the proposed solutions, not all provincials would enter a general congregation ex officio. Still, it did not seem possible to reduce the number of members of a congregation if every single one of the provincials should have to enter ex officio or else the proportion of those sent by the provinces through election would be too greatly reduced with respect to the total number of members. The matter, as was well known, has importance, not only in itself, but also because it is a question of change in the Constitutions, n. 682 ("To give some method of procedure . . . three will come from each province: the provincial and two others chosen by the other participants in the province congregation.").

For this reason, in the end, a solution was approved that stabilizes the number of members in a congregation (about 200) and reduces it slightly (by comparison with the actual number, which has been more or less 230, for a congregation to handle substantial matters) and at the same time excludes very few provincials of provinces (a smaller number than those who are currently provincials of independent vice-provinces) from participation by virtue of office.[13]

As far as those members of the general curia are concerned who participate in a general congregation by virtue of office, the congregation wished to have also the general counselors who are not general assistants and the regional assistants enter as electors ex officio, and did not wish that a limit should be imposed by law on the number of members of the curia who enter ex officio as electors.

---

[13] See D. 3, p. 66f. below.

The congregation also took up certain other points of the Formula of the General Congregation.[14] Moreover, it empowered Father General to change some parts of the Formula that have to do with the handling of substantive issues, in virtue of the authority of the Thirty-third General Congregation if necessary, in the preparation of efficient methods and procedure for a future general congregation.[15]

17. On Poverty

(From the Minutes, Acta 23, 29, 36, 38)

At the time the Thirty-second General Congregation was updating the norms of our poverty by its Decree 12, it wished that the text should be submitted ad cautelam to the Holy See on certain points (especially that communities could be the juridical subjects of apostolic institutes attached to them) that touch the Formula of the Institute in some manner. The Holy See replied, however, that the Decree could take effect "experimentally," "so that the next general congregation may examine the question completely in the light of experience that will be had in the years ahead."[16] The Thirty-third General Congregation, therefore, had to treat the matter once again.

Father Delegate sent questions on Decree 12 of the Thirty-second General Congregation to the province congregations on December 31. The Preparatory Committee examined the replies received from practically every province. It concluded that from the experience in hand it would seem that the decree should be confirmed without change. A special committee composed of Fathers Adolfo Bachelet (Italy), Francisco Egaña (Loyola), Johannes G. Gerhartz (Northern Germany), Eugen Hillengass (Upper Germany), and Urbano Navarrete (Aragon) reached the same conclusion.

Once again the commission set up in the congregation examined the replies and all the postulates. It seemed clear to it that the norms introduced by the Thirty-second General Congregation should be confirmed even though some doubted the experience in hand was sufficiently protracted. The matter was discussed in plenary session and the congregation decreed that the confirmation should possess a definitive character, so long as the Holy See itself confirmed it.[17]

At the same time, it seemed necessary to recall to the minds of all Jesuits the first part of Decree 12 of the Thirty-second Congregation concerning

---

[14] D. 4, see p. 68f. below.

[15] Ibid.

[16] Cf. "Letter of the Cardinal Secretary of State to Father General," May 2, 1975 (AR 16:459). Cf. the letter of Father Arrupe to Pope Paul VI concerning the Decree on Poverty from GC 32 (AR 16:711–19).

[17] D. 2, see p. 65 below.

the spirit of our poverty and its other practical aspects. However, some wished that many points of this sort should be treated once more, others that only a small number should be stressed. When an indicative vote had been taken, paragraphs on "life in poverty" were drafted that succeeded in gaining their own place, finally, in the document "Companions of Jesus Sent into Today's World" (nn. 23–27). They insist on a deeper assimilation of evangelical poverty and on its application. Mention is made also of the spirit of gratuity that is proper to our Institute, a matter that must always be kept in mind, in accordance with the wishes of the Holy See, in choosing ministries.

18. On the Attitude of the Society Toward the Church and Its Hierarchy

(From the Minutes, Acta 20, 34, 38)

A statement on the attitude of our Society toward the Church and its hierarchy holds first place in the "unique document."

The congregation was led to make this statement on several counts. More than once in recent years the popes have addressed the Society on this matter and commended to us full fidelity. The congregation itself was conscious both of defects which have come about in certain circumstances in recent years as well as of the great, even heroic, fidelity of so many Jesuits toward the Church and the Roman pontiff. Finally, there were quite a few postulates urging the congregation to treat this topic.

At the same time, however, the congregation understood that it could not handle, by itself, all the special questions or difficulties and tensions that today's apostolate in this field commonly carries with it. Therefore, it wished to entrust to Father General the task of making further determinations insofar as it will be necessary to do so, and to commend to him special attention with regard to this aspect of our life and activity. In general, the congregation desired to express forthrightly the Society's full insertion in the Church and its wish to serve the Church according to the words of the Second Vatican Council "in its doctrine, life and cult."

19. On Our "Life in the Spirit"

(From the Minutes, Acts 17, 30, 38)

Several postulates were received from the provinces concerning spiritual life in the Society. The Sovereign Pontiff, moreover, strongly recommended to us a deep life in the Spirit. The congregation, therefore, judged it opportune to undertake an evaluation of recent advances as well as deficiencies in attending to the spiritual life. It seemed to the congregation that a renewal is under way and also that this is on account of an impulse given to many Jesuits by recent

apostolic orientations ("option for faith and justice, service of the poor, participation in their life").

This renewal, nevertheless, must be pursued with all vigor. In the first
place, therefore, the congregation wished, rather than undertaking a new
treatment of the whole of our spiritual life, to insist again on integration of
spiritual life and apostolate, which without doubt demands a regular practice of
personal prayer. Then it underscored regular recourse to spiritual discernment,
and finally all-out abnegation that should reveal itself in very concrete aspects of
our life (in availability, in a definite regularity of life, in transcending
individualism).

At the end of its statements on "Life in the Spirit," the congregation
made special recommendation of the summary "On Religious Life in the Society
of Jesus" edited by Father Arrupe in 1975 at the request of the Thirty-second
General Congregation.[18]

20. On the Coadjutor Brothers

(From the Minutes, Acts 14, 24, 32, 35, 36)

The congregation received from the Official Preparatory Committee a
rather full draft document on the brothers that endeavored to respond to a
variety of petitions (e.g., on the specific identity of the vocation, on the lack of
vocations) contained in the postulates. Still both the commission and the
congregation itself experienced some difficulty in handling these questions. It
seemed best that it should not attempt to enter into overly specialized theological questions about which a great difference of opinions and formulations is
evident. On the contrary, the congregation experienced no hesitancy on
essential points, especially on the very great importance of both the religious life
and the work of the brothers in our Society, on continuing efforts toward
fraternal equality among all members, on improving still more the formation of
brothers, on expanding still more their participation in the apostolate.

The congregation wished, therefore, to set these matters before the
whole Society in a spirit of candor and trust. The sentence that expressed fully
the decisive conviction of the congregation, in a direct line with Father Arrupe's addresses, is this: "The Society needs the brothers, first of all for themselves
and then for their labors, for the sake of both its community life and its
apostolate." At the same time the congregation underscored the complementari-

---

[18] *AR* 16:632ff.; paragraphs on "Life in the Spirit" can be found below under n. 9–14
of Decree 1, p. 45–48.

ty of the work of the brothers to those tasks that are properly the work of priests.[19]

Some consideration was given to the question of whether or not the three essential vows of religion, aside from the fourth vow, might become the same for all members, including the brothers.

In the end, the congregation did not wish to debate the question of whether Father General should be directed to begin a study of this matter with a view to a declaration in a future congregation. But Father General himself stated that among the topics concerning the life and vocation of the brothers that he would have to submit to a more profound study, there would have to be included the question of the comparability of the three vows so as to see whether and in what way a change on that point could help in the solution of the general problem (cf. Minutes 36/5).

21. On the Formation of Jesuits

(From the Minutes, Acta 19, 31, 36, 38)

The Official Preparatory Committee was in favor of a very brief statement about formation within the Society. In the end the general congregation issued an even shorter text. It did so, however, only after careful consideration of the situation with the help of a commission and on its own, and having taken account of the Supreme Pontiff's insistence on solid spiritual and intellectual formation.

It was seen that real progress had been brought about in this respect within the Society in recent years. Moreover, Father General had recently promulgated new General Norms of Studies, and new regional orders of studies had been approved for almost all regions. These would seem to be sufficient to enable us to meet the formation needs for our mission. It seemed opportune, therefore, to insist on their execution rather than to add new norms. The heart of the statement[20] is found in these words: "We need solid religious training, serious studies and genuine integration into the apostolic body of the Society."

Although it wished to make no mention of this point in its statement, the congregation did treat also of the possibility of some directory on other aspects of formation besides the program of studies. It was anxious to insist on the integration needed between the spiritual, communitarian and apostolic aspects of formation, and also on the need to promote continuing formation. It concluded by inviting Father General to examine, in dialogue with the assistants, the possibility and opportuneness of editing some kind of "Directory of

---

[19] D. 1, n. 17 ("Life in Communion with the Coadjutor Brothers," n. 15–19), see p. 48 below.

[20] D. 1, n. 20–22, see p. 50f. below.

Formation" which would gather together principles of the Society's tradition with regard to aspects of formation that are not treated in the General Norms of Studies, and with regard to the integration of its various dimensions and different stages.

22. On Our Mission

(From the Minutes, Acta 18, 22, 33)

From the very beginning of the congregation, it was foreseen that the question of apostolic mission would hold a central place in the deliberations. This stems certainly from the very nature of our Society which is established on mission. Moreover, recent circumstances made some sort of evaluation of our apostolate even more necessary at the time of this congregation.

The orientations given by the Thirty-second General Congregation in its Decree 4, "On Our Mission Today: The Service of Faith and the Promotion of Justice" (along with Decree 2, "Jesuits Today") have had an exceedingly deep influence. The idea of the promotion of justice as "an absolute exigency" of the service of faith, in which the mission of the Society consists, had an especially great impact.[21] In general, these thrusts were positive both in our universal apostolate as well as in our spiritual life. At the same time, however, unilateral tendencies occasionally revealed themselves in the application of Decree 4 of the Thirty-second General Congregation. John Paul II had several times lately referred to this in remarks he addressed to us.[22] As far back as 1975, the secretary of state had sent us some special words of exhortation on the proper application of Decrees 2 and 4 of the Thirty-second General Congregation.

In these circumstances it is not surprising that the greater number of all the postulates sent to the general congregation called for both the confirmation of the apostolic orientations given by the last general congregation and also the clarification of certain points (e.g., on the relationship between faith and justice, on the sense of justice that we ought to foster, on the activities proper to Jesuits as priests and religious or, on the contrary, less proper, and so forth). At the same time, a good many were asking that, in the field of the promotion of justice, the general congregation should draw the Society's attention to many very grave problems of the present moment in the area of the preservation of human rights and the fostering of international peace.

---

[21] GC 32, D. 4, n. 2.

[22] "Allocution to the Fathers Provincials," Feb. 27, 1982, n. 8 (*AR* 16:728f.); "Homily to the Members of the 33rd General Congregation," September 2, 1983 (see p. 82 below, n. 7). Cf. also the Directives given by Father Delegate, March 25, 1982: "I. The Apostolate of the Society" (*AR* 18:791-93).

At the same time, there were expectations of a clear confirmation of the importance of the educational and intellectual apostolates as well as research. Some felt that in certain sectors of the Society these had enjoyed less esteem after the Thirty-second Congregation. There was also a wish for an intensification of collaboration with the laity and the confirmation and renewal of different traditional apostolates of the Society.

Both the Preparatory Committee and the commission in the congregation worked hard at examining and discussing all these matters. One thing emerged in the course of these efforts and received confirmation by an indicative vote on October 1: a wish for a quite brief statement that would contain directive guidelines, criteria, and a listing of new fields of apostolate, and, under another aspect, that would take off from a consideration of the wishes of the Supreme Pontiff concerning the Society's apostolate.

In that same indicative vote the congregation expressed a wish for some evaluation, but of a general nature, regarding the application of Decree 4 of the Thirty-second General Congregation. It also called for sobriety in setting forth theological and spiritual guidelines. Finally it wished that the remaining matters (e.g., new fields of the apostolate or the confirmation of traditional ministries) should be treated very briefly, i.e., by way of enumeration, with an exception made for the apostolate of education and research.

All this explains the nature of the statement—contained in the second part of the "unique document"—that the congregation offers to the Society for the direction of our general activities in the years immediately ahead. There is first an evaluation of past experience (nn. 31–33). After that comes the consideration of pressing needs stemming from the condition of the world (nn. 34–36). Then the congregation recalls the appeals and wishes of the Supreme Pontiff, it accepts them in the name of the Society with a grateful heart and shows itself ready to carry out their full execution (nn. 37f.). At the same time it confirms the apostolic orientations set down by the last two congregations, especially, however, by the Thirty-second General Congregation in its Decree 4 (n. 38). It insists then on certain essential aspects of our way of proceeding (nn. 39–42), on some applications (nn. 43–46), and on some dispositions required for the credibility of our mission (nn. 47–49). The conclusion lays strong stress on the centrality of faith in Christ. The statement is a confirmation of orientations already received, but its primary concern is the "future" (n. 50).

23. On the Closing of the Congregation

(From the Minutes, Acta 34, 40, 42, 43, 44)

Father Joseph Labaj, as has already been mentioned, had to leave the congregation because of increasingly serious illness after the election of the Superior General and general assistants. Three other members, Fathers Michael Buckley (California), Andre Costes (France), and Enrico Mariotti (Italy), received permission to be absent for several days. In the same way Fathers Luis Alvarez-Ossorio (Baetica) and Edmundo Rodriguez (New Orleans) were absent for several days, each in order to attend the funeral of his father. Similarly, Father Jesús Montero Tirado (Paraguay) was absent for a few days in order to attend the funeral of his mother. Two others had to be given permission to depart before the conclusion, but this took place only on October 23, very shortly before the end. On the one hand, the permission that Father Janos Tamas (Hungary) had for visiting outside his native land could not be prolonged; on the other hand, Father Urbano Valero (Castile) had to be present in Madrid to open the academic year. Since Father Bruno Bois (Italy) also had to be absent during the last days because of fatigue and Father Dionisio Sciuchetti (Bahia) had to be absent because of the death of a relative, the members of the congregation, who had numbered 220 at the beginning, totaled 215 toward the end. Father Arrupe, who is counted among those members, could not take an active part in the sessions of the congregation because of the state of his health.

As the end of its labors neared, on October 13 the congregation set October 16 as the last date for introducing new postulates. It did not wish, on the contrary, to settle on the last day of the congregation as early as October 13, even though a determination of this sort had been requested by a motion of order. The congregation decided, however, that the final sessions should be expedited by a change in the practice with regard to time allowed for speaking. Thus anyone who asked permission to speak in writing had it for five minutes (instead of seven), and those who asked by flicking on their red light could speak only for three minutes (instead of five).

On October 21 the congregation empowered Father General to see to the proper completion of the legislative work of the congregation insofar as necessary. It also empowered him to suppress colleges and professed houses until the next general congregation and to approve the Acta of the last sessions as well as to make necessary corrections and polish up the style before promulgating the decrees of the congregation. Additional powers were granted him that seem to be required at this time on account of the new codification of Canon Law to ensure the possibility either of requesting certain dispensations from the

Holy See or of adopting or filling out our law in accord with the demands of the new code.[23]

All voting on the document "Companions of Jesus Sent into Today's World" was completed on October 24. The congregation wished, however, that time be left, should it be needed, for presenting intercessions. The last session, therefore, of the congregation took place on October 25 in the afternoon. It was in this session that the Thirty-third General Congregation declared itself ended. The hymn *Te Deum* was chanted in the *aula* and immediately after this session a Eucharistic concelebration was held in the curia chapel. Father General announced that this concelebration would be in thanksgiving most especially for Father Paolo Dezza, as well as for Father Giuseppe Pittau and the former general assistants. He added that the general congregation had reaped the fruits that Father Dezza had sowed by insisting chiefly on the union of our whole Society. Before the Communion, all renewed the consecration of the Society to the Sacred Heart of Jesus according to a formula introduced by Father Arrupe.

Finally, after supper, there was a social gathering in which many artistic and comic talents were put on display. In both the last session of the congregation and the final Eucharistic concelebration, as well as in that recreation after supper, Father General had occasion to express thanks to all whose assistance had been a big aid to the congregation.

24. Some Other Points to Be Noted

On three occasions all the members of the congregation concelebrated a Eucharistic liturgy under the presidency of Father General: September 16, i.e., three days after his election; October 15 in the Basilica of St. Peter's as pilgrims of the Holy Year of Redemption; and finally the last day, as just mentioned. On other days different groups celebrated the Eucharist in different languages in several chapels of the curia and of the House of Writers.

Before each plenary session of the congregation there was a fifteen-minute period of prayer under the leadership of one of the congregation's members.

Just as the Supreme Pontiff, John Paul II, had done at the beginning, so too afterwards, on October 17, the prefect of the Sacred Congregation for Religious, Cardinal Eduardo Pironio, visited the congregation and spoke to the members both about the Synod of Bishops and religious life at the present moment as well as about what the Church expects of our Society.

The congregation lasted for 54 days. There were 43 plenary sessions held in the *aula*. The congregation frequently made use of assistancy groups, but did not have recourse to another type of small meetings, namely, language groups.

---

[23] D. 6, see p. 71–73 below.

APPENDIX A

A LETTER OF VERY REVEREND FATHER GENERAL
PETER-HANS KOLVENBACH
TO THE WHOLE SOCIETY

Dear Brothers in Christ,

P.C.

1. In 1984 I asked Superiors and Province Consultors to tell me of the Society's reaction to the 33rd General Congregation in place of the usual *ex officio* letters. I am now able to communicate to the whole Society the response to that request. More than 1500 letters, about 70% of the number due, plus numerous conversations and many meetings at all levels have contributed to this report on the Society's reception of the most recent General Congregation. This opens up certain perspectives on the future which deserve our close attention.

Return to normal government and to our mission

2. Throughout the Society there was unanimous favorable response to the first result of the General Congregation, that is, the return to normal government. This return was made possible by the deep-seated unity of the delegates which some had expected to be difficult, if not impossible, to achieve. It brought to an end a period of questioning and disquiet, and it returned confidence in the Society as an apostolic body capable of continually rediscovering the demands of the Ignatian charism in response to the challenges put to us by the Holy See and by our age—capable as well of appropriating in all its fullness the spiritual heritage of the last General Congregations and of Father Pedro Arrupe. The return to normal government was accompanied by unanimous grateful recognition of the clearsighted way in which Father Paolo Dezza and his coadjutor Father Giuseppe Pittau carried out their demanding and delicate mission. It also entailed Father Pedro Arrupe's resignation and a public expression of our deep gratitude. But the best way to express gratitude to Father Arrupe will, without a doubt, be to put into effect this exhortation of the 33rd General Congregation: "We believe there is more need at the moment to put into practice what has already been asked of us than to produce extensive

---

This letter, "The Society's Reception of the Thirty-Third General Congregation," appeared in *Acta Romana* 19, no. 2 (1985): 243-56.

declarations or new decrees. For 'love shows itself in deeds rather than in words'" (Decree I, 4).

3. As far as the second result of the General Congregation is concerned, that is, the elaboration and approval of six decrees, only Decree I, entitled "Companions of Jesus Sent into Today's World," has evoked any reactions. For the most part they are positive. To the extent that the 33rd General Congregation accepted as its task "to verify, specify more accurately and confirm the orientations given by General Congregations 31 and 32 in the light of the Church's teaching and the exhortations addressed to us by recent Popes" (Decree I, 2), a favorable reception was to be expected.

4. For the Society's delegates to the 33rd General Congregation, "to avoid erring in the path of the Lord" (Const., n. 605), and in full fidelity to the specific vocation of the Society, which is to leave to the sovereign pontiff the distribution of missions (Const., n. 603), have translated into a language proper to the Society the missions which His Holiness, John Paul II, in his own name and in the name of his predecessors, had just recalled at the opening of the 33rd General Congregation. These missions are: an urgent call vigorously to resist atheism in all its forms of unbelief and false belief; cooperation in the profound renewal of which the Church has need in the midst of the secularized city; the renovation of so many forms of traditional apostolate according to the various spiritual needs of the present moment; the effort to pursue apostolic initiatives of the 2nd Vatican Council (ecumenism, the Church's dialogue with non-Christian religions and with different cultures); the integration into the Church's evangelizing activity of inculturation and of action for the promotion of justice and of peace. All these missions are to be accomplished "in conformity with our vocation as religious and priests," as members of the Society of Jesus, called to be "men of prayer," "teachers of prayer," "masters of the spiritual life" (Homily of John Paul II, 2 September 1983).

5. After a period of severe trials and sufferings which turned us in on ourselves, the 33rd General Congregation sends the Society once more on mission to announce the gospel to non-believers and to those whose faith is different from ours, more than to the faithful of the Lord's Church. This call to direct our apostolic vision outside the Church and the Society, instead of looking only inside, is all the more remarkable since there is another force at work—one of high apostolic priority—to confirm the faithful and to strengthen the Church herself as a sign for the world. It is remarkable also because all the missions which His Holiness John Paul II recalled to the Society as characteristic of its vocation demand the kinds of research, long-range plans and experiments which can easily be open to misunderstanding and at times even to reproach. Hence the conviction of the 33rd General Congregation that "the more a Jesuit is exposed to situations and structures alien to the faith, the more he must strengthen his own religious identity and his union with the whole

body of the Society as represented by the local community to which he belongs" (Decree I, 33).

Our way of proceeding now

6. This authenticity in our apostolic "way of proceeding" has to be verified constantly in the body of the Society. Numerous reactions to the decrees of the General Congregation show that some Jesuits were expecting from Decree I a more precise and more concrete definition of authentic Jesuit life, especially in the two domains that ensure the authenticity of our mission, its poverty and the practice of discernment.

Poverty and preference for the poor with Christ

7. In order to help the Society in every mission "to proclaim the Good News in poverty," some Jesuits were hoping for a more incisive prophetic word and the adoption of a certain number of concrete measures to bring their daily life and their way of carrying out the works of the Society into conformity with a genuine apostolic poverty. These numerous reactions prove that the Society feels the necessity not only of observing the new legislation on poverty (Decree II), but of living its apostolic mission authentically, not only of leading a life which is materially simple—or indeed austere—but especially of embodying, in its way of being and of possessing things, Ignatian gratuity. To be sure, economic necessity can seem to render this at times impracticable. But Ignatian gratuity can still be fully realized in the spending of oneself, and that completely, "to help souls." Without this spirit of gratuity embodied in the giving and forgiving from which our communities draw their life, in our dedication to the mission received, and in an unselfish apostolic perspective, the Society would be recognizable as a respectable commercial venture or an effective welfare organization, but it would no longer announce the gospel of The Poor Man to the poor.

8. The Society's delegates to the 33rd General Congregation were too much aware of the diversity of cultures and of apostolic situations to run the risk of describing in detail the concrete consequences of the "actual poverty" (Spiritual Exercises, 146) to which "the Divine Majesty" has called us "according to the situations of time and place" (Const., *passim*). In order to be genuine, the working out of what poverty means in concrete detail is entrusted to every Jesuit, at whichever level of the Society he is: general, provincial, or local. Although the General Congregation purposely does not enter into concrete details of an authentic life of apostolic poverty, it lends it a new impetus in applying to the lives of all Jesuits and to every Jesuit ministry (cf. Decree I, 48) the preferential option for the poor which is demanded of us by the Church, as

John Paul II recently recalled in an address to the Roman Curia (December 21, 1984).

9. This step forward in the witness of apostolic poverty is at the same time a return to the Society's sources reflected in the Spiritual Exercises. It is not mere chance that the Exercises contain the rule which considers it to be "always better and more secure in what touches one's person and condition of life to be more sparing and to cut back and to come nearer to our High Priest, our model and rule, who is Christ our Lord" in His manner of serving the Faith and the poor (Spiritual Exercises, 344).

10. The integration of the service of faith and the promotion of justice in one single mission (Decree I, 38) is not just a kind of self-approval to justify maintaining every form of the Society's apostolate in its present state. In one single mission everything has to be integrated. Of course, the 33rd General Congregation has not resolved every theoretical and practical problem, nor has it done away with all the ambiguities that arise, in interpreting the promotion of justice in the service of faith. The recent discussions about the theologies of liberation also show how the Church struggles—and is willing to struggle—to bring more clarity into a domain which is the object of its apostolic preference. Tensions and even polarizations exist in some provinces and in some communities. The incompatibility in principle, so often affirmed by the Church, between priestly ministry and certain social commitments, as well as the insensitivity of civil or religious authorities to the social orientations of the Church, have created more than one regrettable situation of conflict. These painful cases receive widespread attention in the media; they should not, though, make us forget that a much larger number of Jesuits manage to overcome conflict, or put up with its tensions, in order to be able to struggle against all injustice and poverty in the name of the gospel that proclaims the beatitude of poverty.

11. In keeping with its vocation the Society takes as its own the preferential option for the poor. But in so doing it will have to pass through a period of apprenticeship and of genuine experimentation in all sectors of its apostolic activity. For the Society, like the Church, while wholeheartedly committing itself to justice in the service of faith, does not know as yet all the concrete consequences of this for pastoral ministry, for the educational sector and even for the social apostolate. Again and again it will have to evaluate the authenticity of its groping and searching, of its experiences and its efforts to walk down this path which the Church points out to us in her most recent documents.

One thing is certain: the Society's solidarity with the poor has a specific character different from that of a political party, a labor union or a development organization. This is because our option looks to the poor person as one who does not live by bread alone.

While Decree I asserts that possession of the Kingdom is the true wealth of the whole human person, it in no way denies the necessity of a socio-economic commitment in the service of humanity. It does, though, situate this in its own religious perspective. As in all other sectors of the Society's apostolic activity, the necessity of depth in our social work in the service of the poor is evident. It requires long-range planning and an expertise based on in-depth preparation.

12. The care to add "non-exclusive" to the preferential option for the poor intends in no way to diminish its urgency. Rather it underscores the fact that the proclamation of the gospel must be to all. The poor are preferred, but they are not the unique object of evangelization. Back in 1974, Father Arrupe told the Union of Superiors General: "The predilection shown by Jesus Christ for the poor will urge the religious of the future to devote themselves to them more and more, without shutting others out" (30 May 1974). The 32nd General Congregation affirmed: "The mission we are called to share is the mission of the Church itself" (Decree 4, 13). The prayer of Ignatius to be placed with the Son, answered at La Storta, becomes the prayer of the Society to be placed with those who incarnate, in and for His Church, the predilection of Christ.

So let us keep on trying to understand better and to realize ever more in our lives and in our apostolic work all the implications of this preferential option for the poor.

Apostolic discernment: difficult and necessary

13. The other point, indispensable for the Society's apostolate, on which a number of Jesuits wanted to see much more precision and practicality, is that of apostolic discernment: the only way to work in constant fidelity to the voice of the Spirit in and for His Church.

The 33rd General Congregation insists particularly on an abiding attitude of discernment without which the whole process of discernment elaborated by the preceding General Congregation remains meaningless. But, to listen to the Society's reactions in this area, Decree I is still too abstract. It sidesteps a concrete confrontation with the problems which immobilize all apostolic impulse and apparently condemn all apostolic discernment to remain a dead letter. These problems, these paralyzing factors, are well known at the provincial level almost everywhere. They go by the name of advancing age, lack of vocations, the burden of traditional obligations and increasing lack of competent manpower. On the community level they often show up as inability to communicate, deep-seated individualism, overwork, unwillingness to work together with others and a refusal to look reality in the face.

14. It is true that the General Congregation cannot furnish practical answers or easy solutions—if there are any—for the concrete problems which apostolic discernment brings up. But it insists on the necessity of discernment "if we are to hear and respond to the call of God in this kind of world . . .".

(Decree I, 12), in order to fulfill our mission (cf. Decree I, 30). While leaving to the apostolic body of the Society at each level of its government, general, provincial and local, the task of determining concretely how to engage in apostolic discernment, the General Congregation in no way justifies inaction or indecision. But it wants to see a process of discernment at work at the crisis points where the very existence and future of the Society's apostolate are at stake.

15. In fact, the Society has reacted already in a practical way to this invitation: the provinces are seeking to establish some kind of apostolic planning with a view to the future. This is not just a measure inspired by common sense for a multi-national organization which, after losing more than 10,000 workers in 20 years while watching the number of its obligations grow, finds itself in the position of having to cut back its activities. Rather, apostolic discernment is a reflection in the context of prayer on the human reality actually at hand. This reality is examined as clearly and objectively as possible, in the light of faith in the Spirit and in the Spirit's Church, so that we may establish within the unchanging apostolic demands of the Society's charism the future orientations to which the Spirit calls us, in and for His Church.

16. These orientations are translated into so many choices among desirable apostolic activities and so many decisions to renew or to close or to open apostolic works. In certain provinces it is a matter of regaining more apostolic mobility. In other places the provinces must prepare themselves to receive a new generation of Jesuits, fewer in number but wholly motivated by the challenges addressed by the Church to the recent General Congregations. In still other places the socio-political circumstances completely restrict apostolic freedom, but they must not be allowed to hinder an indispensable interior renewal. Everywhere, in the most diverse forms, the Society is preparing itself for the apostolic future, the shape of which had been forecast and sketched out by the 2nd Vatican Council and the most recent General Congregations.

17. Whatever remains aloof from this movement of the Spirit will disappear. On the other hand, the apostolic work which enters into it by means of apostolic discernment, recapturing thereby the moment of election in the Spiritual Exercises, ratifies the Society's incorporation into the paschal work of the Lord who died in order to rise again. By means of prayer and communal deliberation, of vision and apostolic administration, of consultation and decision in the Ignatian understanding of government, we have to undergo "a gradual assimilation of that apostolic pedagogy of St. Ignatius." We have to do this if we are to abandon our habitual way of "absolutizing our perceptions and actions." We have to do it if we are to be open to "the newness of Jesus the Savior" bringing to fulfillment in our history the paschal mystery present in everyone who has been called to live the true life and to bear fruit in abundance (cf. Decree I, 13 and 41).

Other challenges

18. Responding concretely to the 33rd General Congregation, the reactions of the Society have not only underscored the apostolic planning that the provinces have to adopt. They have also highlighted, in a particularly vivid way, the following points:

The need for each Jesuit to regain apostolic openness in his life and in his work, by establishing for himself or requesting from his superiors "a rhythm of life which . . . gives us space for solitude and silence, as well as for necessary relaxation and joyous celebration within our communities" (Decree I, 13).

Readiness for a frank and sincere collaboration within the Society, at a time when individualism and particularism still leave so many possibilities unexploited; readiness too for the same kind of apostolic collaboration with the laity, who have already been responsible for a new apostolic impulse in so many of our works.

The will to receive into the Society those whom the Spirit is calling to it but who, perhaps, do not recognize their vocation because of our failure to promote apostolic vocations or because the witness of our lives is obscure or lacking entirely.

The rediscovery of the apostolic vocation of the Brothers in the Society, without which the Society is the poorer in religious and apostolic life.

The need—itself an apostolic one—for in-depth formation, both initial and ongoing, which no consideration should ever compromise, so that we may provide the Church, in whatever form of apostolate, a service of excellence, a "greater" service.

To serve the Lord and the Church wholeheartedly

19. Still another challenge of the 33rd General Congregation which finds a response everywhere is the insistence on the ecclesial character of the Society. Taking up again the leitmotiv of the "rules for gaining the sense of the Church" which is for Ignatius the desire to grow in "communion" with the Church, the General Congregation in its turn wants to see "the entire Society seek to incorporate itself more and more vigorously and creatively in the life of the Church so that we may experience and live its mystery within ourselves" (Decree I, 8). To be frank, insistence on the ecclesial dimension of the Society's apostolate has aroused varied reactions. Some have seen it as a tactical gesture to improve relations with the Holy See. But the great majority recognize in it Ignatius' own dramatic stance toward "nuestra madre" the Church.

20. The same Ignatius who had a long personal experience of conflict and friction with the ecclesiastical authorities in Alcala and in Salamanca, in Jerusalem and in Paris, in Venice and even in Rome, shares the love of the Father for the visible body of His Son in history. Ignatius believes in the mystical unity of the Spirit with the Church, a unity which does not destroy the radical difference between the Spirit and the Church. And because of that belief Ignatius knows no other point of contact with the radical immediacy of God, and no other window onto what the Spirit of Christ sees, than the Church itself. This faith in the Spirit Who raises up the Society for the Church and this faith in the Church which recognizes in the Society the Spirit at work, could never, for Ignatius, be in contradiction to one another. For the Church of the Lord and the prophetic vocation of the Society on behalf of this Church are always of "the same Spirit" (Spiritual Exercises, 365).

21. For this reason we find among the first companions of Ignatius, not an attitude of servile submission, but a spirit that is always constructive, always "building up the Church" in the Pauline sense. This spirit found expression in a service given unconditionally yet prudently, in a readiness to help that was at once loyal and sober, particularly in relation to the Vicar of Christ. Thus Father Polanco was able to write to Father Madrid: "If the members of the Society are papists, they are so in those matters in which they ought to be and in no others, and only in the interests of God's glory and the common good" (Mon. Nadal, II, 263).

22. Faithful to the desire of Ignatius to keep growing in communion with the Church, the General Congregation asks that the whole Society make an effort to "experience" the mystery of the Church and gain an interior understanding of the Church (cf. Decree I, 8). To this fidelity Father Pedro Arrupe also bore witness when he affirmed: "As life goes on and as you penetrate more deeply the mystery of the Church and the charism of the Society, you grow aware with greater conviction that the true *raison d'être* of the Society lies in the service of the Roman Pontiff. To fail in this regard would be to sign our own death sentence. It is, rather, a reason for consolation to see how the Society endeavors always to be as faithful as possible to the Spouse of Christ and to His Vicar" (Homily of 15 January 1977).

23. An ecclesial sense makes us understand how widespread an influence the Society can have in the "building up" of the Lord's Church. It reminds us also that no Jesuit is alone and no work of the Society is isolated in its activity. The quality of our apostolic life, the scientific competence of many Jesuits, and the trust which so many Jesuits and so many of our works inspire in the Church, reflect back upon the whole of the apostolic body of the Society. But this apostolic cohesiveness characteristic of the Society also requires each individual to ponder his responsibility before the whole Society and for the Church, as he performs his ministry in word and in writing, whether as a minister of the

Church's liturgy or as a citizen of his country. Each one involves all his companions, and the Society itself involves the Church, for better or for worse. The teaching of the Church should be able to count on a favorable reception among us, in accord with the Ignatian presupposition, and on a positive and constructive critique. Members of the Society could never approve a critique that is systematically negative and destructive, nor any form of irreverence toward ecclesiastical authorities.

24. Without doubt all the tasks which the Church entrusts to us entail risks in their accomplishment. To announce to a world distant from the Church the love of God manifested in Jesus Christ; to do this by means of social commitment and inculturation, dialogue and ecumenism, theological research and pastoral experience—this requires of us initiatives which lay us open to misunderstanding. Let us recognize in this fact still another reason why we must continually center in the apostolic body of the Society itself our mission to be men in the front lines, and another reason for making it clear within the Church itself that we are living out an authentic mission within the Church, a mission given by the Church. This "missionary" openness to a world at a distance from the Church or allergic to the Church will not always be understood by those ecclesiastical movements whose apostolic priority is primarily or exclusively the reinforcement of ecclesiastical structures or the unification of the faithful alone. Fortunately we are encouraged by the fact that His Holiness John Paul II affirmed and confirmed these specific missions of the Society's apostolate at the opening of the 33rd General Congregation.

Conclusion

25. The many reactions to this General Congregation show clearly that it was not just a Congregation of Election which, in addition, was content with confirming the two preceding General Congregations. The first lines of its decrees maintain that the first and sole concern of the Society should be once more its apostolic mission—the Ignatian "help of souls"—in today's world. While ensuring continuity with the past, the General Congregation did not want to freeze the Society in its present state, but rather to free the missionary dynamism which the Spirit has aroused among us on behalf of the Church, provided we live the Ignatian charism authentically. In this dynamic way the Society understands the resignation of Father Pedro Arrupe who in his last message avows:

> my one ideal was to serve the Lord and His Church—with all my heart—from the beginning to the end. . . . I am full of hope, seeing the Society at the service of the one Lord and of the Church, under the Roman Pontiff, the vicar of Christ on earth. May she keep going along this path, and may God bless us with many good vocations of priests and brothers. . . . (3 September 1983)

26. Be assured, dear brothers, of my union with you in prayer and in work so that the Lord give us to understand the apostolic call which the 33rd General Congregation renews, marking a decisive moment full of promise for the Society's future service within and for the Church. To all and each I express my affection in the Lord.

Fifth Sunday before Easter
    [March 3, 1985]

Fraternally yours in Jesus Christ,

Peter-Hans Kolvenbach, S.J.
Præp. Gen.

APPENDIX B

MEMBERS OF THE THIRTY-FIRST GENERAL CONGREGATION
(in alphabetical order)

Presidents:
To May 22, 1965: Rev. Fr. John L. Swain
From May 22, 1965: Very Rev. Fr. Pedro Arrupe
224/226 Members

Name, (Title,) Province	Name, (Title,) Province
Acévez, Manuel (Northern Mexico)	Colli, Giovanni (Turin)
Achaerandio, Aloisius (Central America)	Connery, John R. (Chicago)
de Aldama, José Ant. (Baetica)	Connolly, John F. X. (California)
Aldunate, José (Chile)	Coreth, Emeric (Austria)
Alf, James (Buffalo)	Corrigan, Terrence (England)
Antunes, Manuel (Portugal)	de la Costa, Horacio (Philippines)
Aquino, Antonio (Central Brazil)	Crandell, William A. (New Orleans)
Arcesú, Federico (Antilles)	Craveiro da Silva, Lucius (Portugal)
Arès, Richard (Montreal)	Crick, Francis (Ranchi)
Arminjon, Blaise (Mediterranean France)	Crowther, Emmanuel (Ceylon)
Arroyo, José (Toledo)	Cullum, Leo A. (Philippines)
Arrupe, Pedro (Japan)	Ćurić, Josip (Croatia)
Azcona, Severiano (Spanish Assistant)	D'Souza, Jerome G. (Indian Assistant)
Azevedo, Marcello (Goian ministry)	Dagher, Abdallah (Near East)
Baeza, Francisco Xav. (Castile)	Daley, John M. (Maryland)
Balaguer, Melchior M. (Bombay)	Dargan, Herbert (Hong-Kong)
Barón, Ferdinandus (Eastern Colombia)	De Genova, Louis (Patna)
Barry, Brendan (Ireland)	Del Zotto, Aloysius (Kerala)
Bednarz, Mieczysław (Lesser Poland)	Delchard, Antoine (Northern France)
Beltrão, Pedro (Southern Brazil)	Dezza, Paolo (Venice-Milan)
Birkenhauer, Henry (Detroit)	Diaz de Acebedo, Jesús (Loyola)
Birkhardt, Francis (Far East)	Divarkar, Parmananda C. A. (Bombay)
Blajot, Victor (Bolivia)	Ducoin, George (Atlantic France)
Boylen, John R. (Australia)	Dupont, André (Madagascar)
Braganza, Francis (Gujarat)	Durocher, Romulo (General Treasurer)
Brenninkmeyer, Bernward (Eastern Germany)	Dzierżek, Stefan (Greater Poland)
Bresciani, Carlo (Bahia)	Elizondo, Miguel (Argentina)
Briceño, Eduardo (Eastern Colombia)	Eminyan, Mauritius (Malta)
Bru, Jean (Atlantic France)	Fank, Karl (Upper Germany)
Bulanda, Eduardus (Greater Poland)	Federici, Giulio Cesar (Rome)
Buuck, Friedrich (Lower Germany)	Fernandes, Lawrence (Madurai)
Byrne, Thomas (Subst. English Assistancy)	Fert, Vaclav F. (Proc. Bohemia in dispersion)
Calvez, Jean (Paris)	Fimmers, Augustin (Northern Belgium)
Cardoso, Armando (Central Brazil)	Fiorito, Miguel A. (Argentina)
Carrier, Hervé (Quebec)	Foley, John J. (Wisconsin)

Name, (Title,) Province	Name, (Title,) Province
Ford, John C. (New England)	Laurent, Philippe (Paris)
Fortier, Vitus (Quebec)	Le Blond, John-Mᵃ (Northern France)
Franchimont, Philippe (Southern Belgium)	Le Saint, William P. (Chicago)
Fransen, Piet (Northern Belgium)	Leary, John P. (Oregon)
Freitas, Geraldo (Northern Brazil)	Leite, Antonio (Portugal)
Fruscione, Salvatore (Sicily)	Lemieux, Albert A. (Oregon)
Fuček, Jan Gualb. (Croatia)	Litva, Felix (Slovakia)
Gallen, Joseph F. (Maryland)	Maas, Simon (Netherlands)
Ganss, George E. (Missouri)	MacDougall, Angus I. (Upper Canada)
García Manrique, Eusebio (Aragon)	Mackenzie, Roderick (Upper Canada)
Gargiulo, Armando (Naples)	Madurga, Mariano (Aragon)
Gentiloni, Filippo (Rome)	Maher, William (England)
van Gestel, Petrus (German Assistant)	Mailleux, Paul (Deleg. for Byzantine Rite)
Giampieri, Alberto (Naples)	Mann, Edward (Bombay)
Giuliani, Maurice (Paris)	Marcozzi, Vittorino (Elect. Venice-Milan)
Gomes, Charles (Goa-Pune)	Markaitis, Bruno (Proc. Lithuania in dispersion)
Gómez Pérez, Raphael (Southern Mexico)	
González, Emmanuel (Japan)	Martegani, Giacomo (Italian Assistant)
González, Guilliermo (Eastern Colombia)	Martinsek, Francis L. (Patna)
González, Luis (Toledo)	Mazón, Candido (Aragon)
Gordon, Ignatio (Baetica)	McCarthy, Charles (Far East)
Goussault, Jacques (Atlantic France)	McGinty, John I. (New York)
Gríful, Isidoro (Uruguay)	McGrail, John A. (Detroit)
Guaschetti, Carlos (Turin)	McMahon, John I. (New York)
Gutiérrez M., Enrico (Southern Mexico)	McQuade, James I. (Detroit)
Harvey, Julien (Quebec)	Mejía, Francisco Xav. (Western Colombia)
Hirschmann, Johannes (Lower Germany)	Mertens, Victor (Central Africa)
Hogan, Jeremiah (Australia)	Messineo, Antonio (Sicily)
Hoing, Iosef (Northern Belgium)	Mirewicz, Jerzy (Greater Poland)
Hughes, Lachlan (Salisbury)	Monachino, Vicenzo (Rome)
Iglesias, Ignacio (León)	Monteiro, Sylvester (Karnataka)
Iriarte, Victor (Venezuela)	Moreno, Alberto (Northern Latin American Assistant)
Iturrioz, Iesús (Loyola)	
Junk, Nicolaus (Lower Germany)	Mruk, Antoni (Lesser Poland)
Kelley, John I. (Oregon)	Mueller, Ansgar (Southern Brazil)
Kelly, Francis P. (Australia)	Murphy, William I. (New England)
Kerr, John (Ireland)	Murray, John (England)
Klein, Heinrich (Eastern Germany)	Naughton, James W, (Secr. Soc.)
Klubertanz, George P. (Wisconsin)	O'Brien, Joseph D. (Calfornia)
Kozèlj, Jan B. (Croatia)	O'Connor, John V. (New England)
Kušmierz, Antony (Lesser Poland)	O'Connor, Paul L. (Chicago)
Lacourt, Francçois (Northern France)	O'Conor, Charles (Ireland)
Lang, Cecil E. (New Orleans)	O'Keefe, Vincent T. (New York)
Laramée, Jean (Montreal)	Ochagavia, Juan (Chile)
Larrain, Ferdinando (Chile)	d'Oncieu, Eugene (Mediterranean France)

Name, (Title,) Province	Name, (Title,) Province
Oñate, Iosé (East Asian Assistant)	Shea, Arthur F. (Philippines)
Orie, Carolus (Indonesia)	Sheridan, Edward (Upper Canada)
Pasupasu, Daniel (Central Africa)	Silva, Francisco (California)
Pillain, Etienne (French Assistant)	Simmel, Ansgar (Upper Germany)
Pinsker, Anton (Austria)	Small, Harold O. (American Assistant)
Portilla, Enrico (Southern Mexico)	Smith, Andrew C. (New Orleans)
Pujol, Clemens (Tarragona)	Smulders, Piet (Netherlands)
Ramírez, Eduardo (Western Colombia)	Soballa, Gunther (Eastern Germany)
Reed, John I. (Buffalo)	de Sobrino, José (Baetica)
Reinert, Paul C. (Missouri)	Sogni, Aemilio (Turin)
Renard, Aloisius (Southern Belgium)	Sponga, Edward A (Maryland)
Rentería, Ignacio (Northern Mexico)	Swain, John L. (Vic. Gen., English Assis-
Riaza, José M. (Castile)	tant)
Ribas, Pedro (Tarragona)	von Tattenbach, Franz (Upper Germany)
Richard, Jean (Montreal)	Tejerína, Angel (León)
Ridruejo, José (Peru)	Terpstra, Jan (Netherlands)
Roberts, Anthony P. (Jamshedpur)	Thomas, John L. (Wisconsin)
Robinson, Francisco (Northern Mexico)	Thro, Linus I. (Missouri)
Rocha, Juan B. (Southern Latin American	Tobin, Denis T. (Jamaica)
Assistant)	Troisfontaines, Roger (Southern Belgium)
Romañá, Antonio (Taragona)	Tucci, Roberto (Naples)
Rondet, Michel (Southern France)	Ugarte, Emilio (Madurai)
Rosa, Leo (Venice-Milan)	Van Roey, Lawrence (Ranchi)
Rosenlelder, Richard M. (Patna)	Varaprasadam, John Mª (Madurai)
de Roux, Rodolfo (Western Colombia)	Varga, Andrew (Hungary)
Ryex, Mauritius (Central Africa)	Vélaz, José Emman. (Loyola)
Salaverri, Ioachin (León)	Velloso, Pedro B. (Central Brazil)
Salvo, Hippolytus (Argentina)	Verstraete, Lucas (Ranchi)
Schasching, Johann (Austria)	Villalba, Alfonso (Equador)
Schoenenberger, Mario (Switzerland)	Villanova, Daniele (Sicily)
Segura, Manuel (Paraguay)	Vizmanos, Francisco a B. (Castile)
Sehnem, João B. (Southern Brazil)	Voss, Gustave (Japan)
Shan, Paul (Far East)	Wautier, Albert (Calcutta)
Shanahan, James I. (Buffalo)	

MEMBERS OF THE THIRTY-SECOND GENERAL CONGREGATION
(In Alphbetical Order)

President: Very Rev. Fr. Pedro Arrupe
Elected General on May 22, 1965
(236 Members)

Name, (Title,) Province	Name, (Title,) Province
Abellán, Pedro (Proc. Gen., Toledo)	Calvez, Jean-Yves (Gen. Asst., Atlantic France)
Acévez, Manuel (Reg. Asst., Mexico)	
Achaerandio, Luis (Central America)	Casassa, Charles (California)
Adám, John (Hungary)	Chabert, Henri (Southern France)
Adami, Leopoldo (Southern Brazil)	Chu, Bernard (China)
Agúndez, Melecio (Castile)	Clancy, Thomas (New Orleans)
Aizpun, José (Gujarat)	Clarke, Thomas (New York)
Aldecoa, José Antonio (Loyola)	Cleary, Richard (New England)
Alfaro, Juan (Loyola)	de Colnet, Yves (Northern France)
Alvarez-Bolado, Alfonso (Castile)	Connery John (Chicago)
Amet, Henri (Atlantic France)	Connor, James (Maryland)
Antunes, Manuel (Portugal)	Coreth, Emerich (Austria)
Arango, Gerardo (Colombia)	Correia-Afonso, John (Reg. Asst., Bombay)
Arevalo, Catalino (Philippines)	de la Costa, Horacio (Gen. Asst., Philippines)
Arroyo, José (Toledo)	
Arrupe, Pedro (Superior General, Japan)	Costes, André (All France, Mediterranean France)
Arvesú, Federico (Antilles)	
Athazhapadam, Thomas (Patna)	Counihan, John (Zambia)
Bamberger, Stefan (Switzerland)	Cruz, Luis A. (Ecquador)
Baragli, Enrico (Rome)	Curic, Josip (Croatia)
Barré, Noël (Atlantic France)	Cuyás, Manuel (Tarragona)
Begley, John (Australia)	Daniel, William (Australia)
Belic, Miljenko (Croatia)	Dargan, Herbert (Reg. Asst., Hong Kong)
Berden, Pavel (Slovenia)	Dargan, Joseph (Ireland)
Bergoglio, Jorge (Argentina)	Darowski, Roman (Lesser Poland)
Besanceney, Paul (Detroit)	Decloux, Simon (Southern Belgium)
Biever, Bruce (Wisconsin)	De Cooman, Eugeen (Northern Belgium)
Blanco, Benito (Antilles)	van Deenen, Jan (Netherlands)
Boné, Edouard (Southern Belgium)	De Hovre, Luk (Northern Belgium)
Bortolotti, Roberto (Rome)	De Mello, Anthony (Bombay)
Botturi, Tarcisio (Bahia)	Dezza, Paolo (Gen. Asst., Venice-Milan)
Bourgeault, Guy (French Canada)	Díaz Bertrana, Marcos (Baetica)
Brenninkmeyer, Bernward (Eastern Germany)	Divarkar, Parmananda (Bombay)
	D'Mello, Ambrose (Karnataka)
Browne, Joseph (New York)	Domínguez, Héctor (Baetica)
Buckley, Michael (California)	Dortel-Claudot, Michel (Northern France)
Cachat, Leo (Patna)	D'Souza, Noel (Calcutta)
	D'Souza, Romuald (Goa-Pune)

Name, (Title,) Province	Name, (Title,) Province
Dullard, Maurice (Ranchi)	Kijauskas, Gediminas (Lithuania)
Echeverría, José Luis (Venezuela)	Knecht, Joseph (Patna)
Egaña, Francisco (Loyola)	Koczwara, Tadeusz (Greater Poland)
Ekka, Philip (Ranchi)	Kolacek, Josef (Bohemia)
Ekwa bis Isal (Central Africa)	Kolvenbach, Peter-Hans (Near East)
Fabbri, Enrique (Argentina)	Krauss, Heinrich (Upper Germany)
Fang Chih-Jung, Marc (China)	Kullu, Patrick (Ranchi)
Farrell, Walter (Detroit)	Kunz, Erhard (Lower Germany)
Fernández, Avelino (León)	Kyne, Michael (England)
Fernández-Castañeda, José Luis (Peru)	Lambert, Louis (New Orleans)
Flaherty, Daniel (Chicago)	Lapize de Salée, Bernard (Southern France)
Fragata, Julio (Portugal)	Lariviere, Florian (French Canada)
Galauner, Petar (Croatia)	Laurendeau, Louis (Secr. Soc., French Canada)
Galbraith, Kenneth (Oregon)	
Ganzi, Igino (Reg. Asst., Turin)	Leão, Joaquim (Mozambique)
Gerhartz, Johannes Günter (Lower Germany)	van Leeuwen, Hans (Netherlands)
Giorgianni, Giovanni (Sicily)	Leite, Antonio (Portugal)
Gnanadickam, Casimir (Madurai)	Lesage, Jacques (Reg. Asst., Paris)
Gordon, Douglas (Madurai)	Londoño, Fernando (Colombia)
Grez, Ignacio (Chile)	Lucey, Paul (New England)
Guidera, John (Jamshedpur)	Macchi, Angelo (Venice-Milan)
Guindon, William (New England)	Mac Gregor, Felipe (Peru)
Gutiérrez, Enrique (Mexico)	Madurga, Mariano (Aragon)
Gutiérrez Semprún, Manuel (Castile)	Mahoney, Martin (New York)
Hall, Bernard (England)	Malone, Patrick (Upper Canada)
Hannan, Michael (Salisbury)	Marranzini, Alfredo (Naples)
Hardawirjana, Robert (Indonesia)	Martini, Carlo (Turin)
Harvanek, Robert (Chicago)	Mayo, Benigno (Philippines)
Harvey, Julien (French Canada)	McCarthy, Charles (China)
Hayashi, Shogo (Japan)	McGarry, Cecil (Ireland)
Hebga, Meinrod (Western Africa)	McPolin, James (Ireland)
Hillengass, Eugen (General Treasurer, Upper Germany)	Meharu, Carlos (Uruguay)
	Menacho, Antonio (Bolivia)
Hoël, Marc (Northern France)	Mendes de Almeida, Luciano (East Central Brazil)
Hoffmann, Georg (Eastern Germany)	
Hortal, Jesús (Southern Brazil)	Mendizábal, Miguel (Japan)
Huarte, Ignacio (Venezuela)	Mertens, Victor (Reg. Asst., Central Africa)
Huber, Eduard (Upper Germany)	
Hughes, Gerard J. (England)	Miecznikowski, Stefan (Greater Poland)
Huizing, Peter (Netherlands)	
Iglesias, Ignacio (Reg. Asst., León)	Mitchell, Robert (New York)
Jiménez, Gustavo (Colombia)	Molinari, Paolo (Turin)
Kaufmann, Leo (Oregon)	Montes, Fernando (Chile)
Kern, Walter (Austria)	Moragues, Ignacio (Aragon)
	Moreland, Gordon (Oregon)

Name, (Title,) Province	Name, (Title,) Province
Dias de Moura, Laercio (Reg. Asst., Central Brazil)	Sheets, John (Wisconsin)
Moysa-Rosochacki, Stefan (Lesser Poland)	Sheridan, Edward (Reg. Asst., Upper Canada)
Mruk, Anton (Reg. Asst., Lesser Poland)	Sily, Alberto (Argentina)
Muguiro, Ignacio (Peru)	Small, Harold (Reg. Asst., Oregon)
Navarrete, Urbano (Aragon)	Soenarja, Antonius (Indonesia)
Ochagavía, Juan (Chile)	Soltero, Carlos (Mexico)
O'Keefe, Vincent (Gen. Asst., New York)	Sorge, Bartolomeo (Venice-Milan)
O'Malley, John (Detroit)	Sucre, Gustavo (Venezuela)
Orsy, Ladislas (New York)	Suradibrata, Paul (Indonesia)
O'Sullivan, Patrick (Australia)	de Survilliers, Alain (Atlantic France)
Padberg, John (Missouri)	Tabao, François-Xavier (Madagascar)
Panuska, Joseph (Maryland)	Taylor, Eamon (New York)
Pasupasu, Daniel (Central Africa)	Tejerina, Angel (León)
Pelenda Bikakala (Central Africa)	Tomé, Mariano (Cuba)
Pereira, Joaquim (East Central Brazil)	Torres Gasset, Juan (Tarragona)
Pérez-Lerena, Francisco (Antilles)	Troisfontaines, Roger (Southern Belgium)
Perniola, Vito (Ceylon)	Tucci, Roberto (Naples)
Perz, Zygmunt (Greater Poland)	Vadakel, Paul (Kerala)
Petrucelli, Donato (Naples)	Valero, Urbano (All Spain (Castile)
Philipps, Bertram (Bombay)	Van Bladel, Louis (Northern Belgium)
Pilz, Johann Chr. (Australia)	Vandermeersch, Edmond (Paris)
Piña, Joaquin (Paraguay)	Vanni, Ugo (Rome)
Popiel, Jan (Lesser Poland)	Varaprasadam, Arul Maria (Madurai)
Prucha, Paul (Wisconsin)	de Varine-Bohan, Jean (Paris)
Rakotonirina, Charles-Remy (Madagascar)	de Vaucelles, Louis (Paris)
Randriambololona, Philibert (Madagascar)	Vaughan, Richard (California)
Rendina, Sergio (Venice-Milan)	Vela, Luis (León)
Roth, Herbert (Eastern Germany)	Vella, Arthur (Malta)
Russell, John (Hong Kong)	Vergnano, Carlo (Turin)
Russo, Biagio (Sicily)	Viard, Claude (Mediterranean France)
Ryan, William (Upper Canada)	Vives, José (Tarragon)
San Juan, Vicente (Philippines)	Walsh, Maurice (Jamaica)
Santana, Hindenburg (Northern Brazil)	Walsh, Terence (Upper Canada)
Sanz Criado, Luis M. (Toledo)	Weber, Leo (Missouri)
Scaduto, Mario (Sicily)	Weber, Quirino (Eastern Brazil)
Schasching, Johann (Reg. Asst., Austria)	Whelan, Joseph (Maryland)
Scheifler, Xavier (Mexico)	Wulf, Friedrich (Lower Germany)
Segura, Manuel (Baetica)	Yamauchi, James (New Orleans)
Seibel, Vitus (Upper Germany)	Yanase, Mutsuo (Japan)
Sencik, Stefan (Slovakia)	Zamarriego, Tomas (Toledo)
Sheahan, Gerald (Missouri)	

MEMBERS OF THE THIRTY-THIRD GENERAL CONGREGATION
(in alphabetical order)

Presidents:
Very Rev. Fr. Pedro Arrupe
Superior General from May 22, 1965
Rev. Fr. Paolo Dezza
Delegate of Pope Paul II from October 5, 1981
Rev. Fr. Giuseppe Pittau
Coadjutor of the Delegate of Pope Paul II
(220 Members)

Name, (Title,) Province

Name, (Title,) Province

Adami, Leopoldo (Southern Brazil)
Agius, Alfred (Malta)
Almeida, Leslie (Goa-Pune)
Alvarez-Ossorio, Luis M. (Baetica)
Amaladoss, Michael (Madurai)
Antolovic, Josip (Croatia)
Araujo, José (Ecuador)
Arnaiz, José (Antilles)
Arroyo, José (Toledo)
Arrupe, Pedro (Superior General, Japan)
Arteaga, José (Chile)
Arza, Antonio (Loyola)
Awamoto, Paul Teruo (Japan)
Acevedo, Marcello de C. (East Central Brazil)
Bamberger, Stefan (Switzerland)
Barre, Noel (France)
Beaudry, Albert (French Canada)
van Beeck, Frans (Netherlands)
Beirle, Theodor (Upper Germany)
Bergoglio, Jorge Mario (Argentina)
Bernas, Joaquin G. (Philippines)
Bertolusso, Vicenzo (Italy)
Bianchini, Sergio (Italy)
Bois, Bruno (Italy)
Brassil, J. Paul (Zambia)
Brenninkmeijer, Gregory (Netherlands)
Browne, Joseph T. (New York)
Buckley, Michael J. (California)
Burns, Patrick J. (Wisconsin)
Byrne, Brendan (Australia)
Calvez, Jean-Yves (Gen. Asst., France)

Campbell-Johnston, Michael (England)
Cardo, Franco Carlos (Peru)
Carlson, Gregory I. (Wisconsin)
Carriere, Bernard (French Canada)
Case, Francis E. (Oregon)
Chang Ch'un-shen, Aloysius B. (China)
Chu Li-Teh, Michel (China)
Chu Meng-Chuan, Bernard (Chinese Apostolate, China)
Clark, John W. (California)
Cooke, Vincent M. (New England)
Corella, Jesús (Castile)
Costes, André (France)
Czerwinski, Josef (Austria)
Damiani, Antonio (Italy)
Danuwinata, Francis X. (Indonesia)
Dargan, Joseph (Ireland)
Darminta, Joseph (Indonesia)
Decloux, Simon (Southern Belgium)
De la Marche, Marc (Northern Belgium)
Delobre, Denis (France)
de Mello, Anthony (Bombay)
Devereux, James A. (Maryland)
Dezza, Paolo (Papal Delegate, Italy)
Diego, Luis de (Venezuela)
Divarkar, Parmananda (Gen. Asst., Bombay)
D'Mello, John F. (Patna)
Doyle, Patrick (Ireland)
D'Souza, Alphonse (Calcutta)
D'Souza, Noel (Calcutta)
Duffy, Paul (Australia)

Name, (Title,) Province | Name, (Title,) Province

Dullard, Maurice (Ranchi)
Durack, Jerome F. (Patna)
Earle, George (England)
Egan, Liam A. (Macao–Hong Kong)
Egaña, Francisco J. (Loyola)
Ellacuría, Ignacio (Central America)
Fang Chih-jung, Mark (China)
Fernandes, Julian (Karnataka)
Fernandes, Stanislaus (Gujarat)
Fernández, Avelino (León)
Fernández-Castañeda, José (Peru)
Fleming, David L. (Missouri)
Flipo, Claude (France)
Fonseca, Michael (Ranchi)
Galauner, Petar (Reg. Asst., Croatia)
Galli, Agide (West Africa)
García, Nelson (Antilles)
García Gomez, Matias (Baetica)
García Hernández Ros, Ramon (Peru)
García Rodríguez, José (Castile)
Gellard, Jacques (France)
Gerhartz, Johannes Günter (Northern Germany)
Gnanadickam, Casimir (Reg. Asst., Madurai)
González Faus, José Ignacio (Aragon)
Gray, Howard J. (Detroit)
Grzebien, Ludwik (Southern Poland)
Guindon, William G. (New England)
Gutiérrez Semprún, Manuel (Uruquay)
Hall, Bernard (Reg. Asst., England)
Harnett, Philip (Ireland)
Harrington, Daniel J. (New England)
Harvanek, Robert F. (Chicago)
Hegyi, Janos (Hungary)
Hennaux, Jean-Marie (Southern Belgium)
Henriot, Peter J. (Oregon)
Hillengass, Eugen (General Treasurer, Upper Germany)
Hughes, Kenneth J. (Jamaica)
Iglesias, Ignacio (Spain)
Jacqmotte, Guy (Northern Belgium)
Javorka, Jozef (Slovakia)
Jerez, César (Central America)
Jeyaraj, Michael (Madurai)

Karekezi, Augustin (Central Africa)
Kavanaugh, John F. (Missouri)
de Kergaradec, Yves (France)
Klein, Alfons (Upper Germany)
Klein, J. Leo (Chicago)
Kokalj, Joze (Slovenia)
Kolvenbach, Peter-Hans (Near East)
Kunz, Erhard (Upper Germany)
Kuriakose, Joseph (Madurai)
Kyne, Michael (England)
Labaj, Joseph J. (Wisconsin)
Lambino, Antonio B. (Philippines)
Laurendeau, Louis (French Canada)
Lavelle, Michael J. (Detroit)
van Leeuwen, Hans (Netherlands)
Lombardi, Federico (Italy)
Londoño, Fernando (Colombia)
Lopez Rosas, Ernesto (Argentina)
Luhmer, Klaus (Japan)
Mac Dowell, João (East Central Brazil)
Madelin, Henri (France)
Mahan, Terrance L. (California)
Mariotti, Enrico (Italy)
Matic, Marko (Croatia)
McGarry, Cecil (Gen. Asst., Ireland)
McGarry, William J. (New York)
Menendez, Valentin (Central America)
Menendez Urena, Enrique (León)
Miyares, José Manuel (Antilles)
Montero Tirado, Jesús (Paraguay)
Montes Fernando (Chile)
Moragues, Ignacio J. (Aragon)
Morujão, Manuel (Portugal)
Munzihirwa Mwene, Ngabo (Central Africa)
Nakai, Makoto (Japan)
Nebres, Bienvenido F. (Philippines)
O'Callaghan, John J. (Chicago)
Ochagavía, Juan (Chile)
O'Donovan, Leo J. (Maryland)
O'Flaherty, Edward M. (New England)
O'Hare Joseph A. (New York)
O'Keefe, Vincent T. (Gen. Asst., New York)
O'Malley, John W. (Detroit)

Name, (Title,) Province	Name, (Title,) Province

O'Neill, Charles E. (New Orleans)
Opiela, Stanislaw (Greater Poland)
Orsy, Ladislas (New York)
O'Sullivan, Patrick (Australia)
Ozog, Eugeniusz (Southern Poland)
Pai, Rex A. (Indonesia)
Pasupasu, Daniel (Central Africa)
Pelka, Florian (Greater Poland)
Pereira, Joaquim (East Central Brazil)
Perz, Zygmunt (Greater Poland)
Pfahl, Rolf-Dietrich (Northern Germany)
Pittau, Giuseppe (Coadjutor, Papal Delegate, Japan)
Plamondon, Louis (Eastern Africa)
Platzgummer, Helmut (Austria)
Plazaola, Juan (Loyola)
Prabhu, John C. (Jamshedpur)
Prendergast, Terrence (Upper Canada)
Puca, Pasquale (Italy)
Pullattu, Mathew (Kerala)
Puthumana, Abraham (Patna)
Rambla, Josep Maria (Tarragona)
Randriambololona, Philibert (Madagascar)
Rasolo, Louis (Madagascar)
Rasquinha, Edwin (Bombay)
Razafintsalama, Adolphe (Madagascar)
Remolina, Gerardo (Colombia)
Restrepo, Alvaro (Colombia)
Riedlsperger, Alois (Austria)
Rocha e Melo, Luis (Portugal)
Rodriguez, Edmundo (New Orleans)
Roeffaers, Hugo (Northern Belgium)
Royce, Thomas R. (Oregon)
Royon, Elias (Toledo)
Rush, Robert T. (Reg. Asst., Japan)
Ryan, William F. (Upper Canada)
Sagi, Janko (Croatia)
Salvat, Ignasi (Tarragona)

Samarasinghe, Ashley (Sri Lanka)
Sanchez del Rio, Luis T. (Toledo)
Santana, Hindenburg (Northern Brazil)
Saulaitis, Antanas (Lithuania)
Sciuchetti, Dionisio (Bahia)
Segura, Manuel (Baetica)
Seibel, Vitus (Upper Germany)
Seron, Eduardo (Aragon)
Servais, Emmanuel (Southern Belgium)
Sheahan, Gerald R. (Reg. Asst., Missouri)
Sheridan, Edward F. (Upper Canada)
Soares-Prabhu, George (Bombay)
Soenarja, Antonius (Indonesia)
Soltero, Carlos (Mexico)
Sosa, Arturo (Venezuela)
Spence, Kenneth (Zimbabwe)
Spidlik, Tomas (Bohemia)
Stahel, Thomas H. (New Orleans)
Steczek, Boguslaw (Southern Poland)
Stellini, Emmanuel (Calcutta)
Swinnen, Andres Maria (Argentina)
Tamas, Janos (Hungary)
Tejerina, Angel (León)
Topno, Pascal (Ranchi)
Trias Bertran, Jorgé (Bolivia)
Tucci, Roberto (Italy)
Ugalde, Luis (Venezuela)
Valero, Urbano (Castile)
Vaz Pato, Manuel (Portugal)
Vergara, Jesús (Mexico)
Vigil Avalos, Carlos (Mexico)
Vives, Josep (Tarragona)
Weber, Ivo P. (Southern Brazil)
Weber, João Quirino (Southern Brazil)
Weber, Leo F. (Missouri)
Whelan, Joseph P. (Maryland)
Wood, William T. (New York)